THE IMPACT OF DEPRESSION ON CHRONIC ILLNESS:

PREVALENCE, RISK FACTORS, SCREENING TOOLS

AND EFFECTIVE TREATMENTS

A Doctoral Project

Presented to the Faculty

School of Behavioral Sciences

California Southern University

By

Valerie S. Brandal, Psy.D.

Acknowledgments

In my current role as a medical social worker for home care and hospice, I visit many patients, most of whom have been diagnosed with at least one chronic illness. Many patients I have seen multiple times over several episodes and I have noticed that several of them struggle with depression and anxiety. It is required that I have a Master of Social Work degree and am licensed by the state. This degree does allow me to provide counseling services; however, in this role as a medical social worker, it is not a service that insurance companies will pay for. They will pay for "skilled" visits which means I must provide instruction to patients about available community resources and make referrals as appropriate.

Over the course of the past seven years as a medical social worker, I have become convinced that depression and anxiety have a significant impact on chronic illness, self-management of chronic illness, and vice versa. It is my contention that, with effective intervention (i.e. counseling), my patients would see improvements in their mental health as well as their physical health. They would see a decrease in the number of hospitalizations, ER visits, doctor's office visits, and exacerbations of their chronic illness. My hope for this doctoral project is that the results would show insurance companies the value of utilizing home care and hospice social workers to provide effective counseling services and change their coverage policies for social work visits.

I would like to thank God for the opportunities and abilities He has provided to me to be able to pursue and complete this doctoral degree. I would like to thank my family and friends who have cheered me on throughout this chapter in my life and their understanding for having to put other activities on hold in order to finish this degree. I would like to express my profound gratitude to Dr. McKiernan (my doctoral project committee chair), Dr. Allen (my doctoral project committee chair and coursework mentor) as well as all the mentors who have provided

feedback in preparation of the Doctor of Psychology
degree.

Doctoral Project Abstract

Title: The Impact of Depression on Chronic Illness: Prevalence, Risk Factors, Screening Tools and Effective Treatments

Author: Valerie S. Brandal

Degree: Doctor of Psychology

Institution: California Southern University

Scope of Study: The relationship between depression and chronic illness is reviewed with concentration on the latest research. The purpose of this paper was to examine the prevalence of depression in patients with chronic illness, discover valid and reliable screening tools, explore potential risk factors for developing depression, and learn about proven effect treatment interventions. An objective of this study involved the review of scholarly journal articles gathered through electronic search engines. The literature included studies conducted only in the United States regarding adults diagnosed with depression and one or more of the top chronic physical illnesses.

Findings and Conclusions: Treatment of depression and

chronic illness cannot be effectively started without first recognizing the prevalence and severity of the problem. The findings of this study revealed that, in 27 studies with 24,000 participants diagnosed with at least one chronic illness, 73.7% met criteria for either major or minor depression. Self-report questionnaires are gaining in popularity and the four most popular screening tools for depression include the Beck Depression Inventory – II (BDI-II), the Center for Epidemiological Studies – Depression (CES-D), the Geriatric Depression Scale (GDS), and the Patient Health Questionnaire, Nine Symptom Checklist (PHQ-9). Several risk factors for developing depression include, but are not limited to, financial strain, social isolation, chronic pain, diagnosis of two or more chronic illnesses, older age, female, and poor health. Only two studies addressed psychological interventions and reported significant changes with the implementation of cognitive behavioral therapy, COPD education, and dyspnea management.

Table of Contents

Chapter One: Introduction

Chronic physical and mental illness is on the rise in America and so is the cost of treatment. For many Americans, legal and illegal residents of the United States, the affordability of health care is out of reach. Over the three years prior to this study, health care and health care reform has been a hot topic of debate and controversy in many arenas of our society, especially with politicians, medical professionals, the media, the current Presidential Administration and most, if not every, household in America. Many talking points of the debate focus on waste and fraud, health care as a right, coverage for everyone, and deciding who should receive treatment and when.

Important issues that have not been but should be considered in the health care debate include the relationship between mental and physical health, the influence of psychological interventions on mental and physical health, and the potential these interventions have to reduce the cost of health care. Statistics from the

Centers for Disease Control and Prevention (CDC) (2009) show that, in 2005, 133 million Americans had at least one chronic illness. More recent data suggests that the prevalence of depression is 7.3% among adults 40 to 59 years of age (Karakus & Patton, 2011). One in four adults (approximately 61.4 million) experience a mental health disorder in any given year, according to the National Alliance on Mental Illness (2013).

Over half (54%) of all depressed patients (with an average age of onset of 32) in primary care settings go undetected (Maradiegue & Khan, 2013). Red flags that put patients at risk for depression include family history of mental illness, poverty, financial strain, significant life changes, pregnancy and post- pregnancy, social isolation, somatic complaints, substance abuse, older age, loss of sex drive, chronic pain, and diagnoses of two or more chronic illnesses. By 2020, it is projected that the prevalence of depression will be second only to heart disease (Chapman, Perry & Strine, 2005) and that it will be the leading cause of disability for women (NAMI, 2011). Helping patients control their depression will also empower them with the ability to control other chronic illnesses (Maradiegue & Khan, 2013). Therefore, it is vital to understand the connection between mental health and physical health.

Background of the Problem

Quality of life is greatly affected by depression and co-occurring chronic physical illness because of the functional limitations that symptoms impose upon individuals. The most frequently diagnosed chronic physical illnesses include arthritis, heart disease, cancer, kidney disease, diabetes, and lung disease. Depression can exacerbate inpatient hospitalizations, frequent doctor's office and emergency room visits, and individual efforts to self-manage chronic physical illnesses. Some studies report that, in younger adults, even a prior history of depression increases the likelihood of poor health, cardiovascular disease, diabetes, metabolic syndrome, and

3

in-hospital mortality (Cho, Lavretsky, Olmstead, Levin, Oxman, & Irwin, 2010). It appears reasonable to assume that appropriate psychological interventions have the potential to reduce the number of visits to the emergency room, hospital, and/or doctor's office while increasing the individual's ability to provide self-care.

Arthritis is the most frequent cause of disability among American adults (Theis, Hemlick & Hootman, 2007). Co-occurring psychological distress appears to affect 5.6% while co-morbid anxiety and depression affects 25.2% of those adults with arthritis. In fact, the prevalence of depression and anxiety is significantly higher for people who have arthritis than for those who do not. The conclusion can be made, then, that early detection, regular mental health assessments and specific interventions will benefit not only individuals with arthritis but also those with other chronic illnesses like heart disease.

According to the CDC ("Heart Disease Facts," 2010), every year 715,000 individuals suffer a heart attack and

190,000 of these individuals have already had at least one previous heart attack. Coronary artery disease (CAD) is the leading cause of death in the U.S. and in the world (Huffman, Smith, Quinn & Fricchione, 2006). The impact of psychological symptoms on heart disease, however, did not get any attention until the 1970's when N. H. Hackett & T. D. Cassem began an investigation. Interest picked up in the 1980's with the work of Friedman et al. when they found that individuals with Type A behaviors had significantly decreased morbidity and mortality after receiving counseling. Changes that occurred as a result of that counseling continued long after the intervention itself had ended. In the 1990's studies conducted by Frasure-Smith found that depressive symptoms (meaning an elevated score of 10 or above on the Beck Depression Inventory) in the first week following a heart attack predicted cardiac death either six or eighteen months later. Treatment of depressive and anxiety symptoms can potentially lead to 15% fewer coronary events, translating to over 100,000 fewer heart attacks and 25,000 fewer cardiac deaths annually.

The second leading cause of death in America is cancer, and, in 2009, an estimated 1,555 people died from cancer every day (CDC, "Cancer Statistics by Cancer Type," 2010). Receiving a diagnosis of a life-threatening illness like cancer creates fear and uncertainty which, in turn, has an impact on quality of life (Franks & Roesch, 2006). A cancer patient may also be dealing with additional psychosocial stressors (outside of the cancer diagnosis) as well as physical limitations which may contribute to increased general distress, anxiety and depression. Physical symptoms of cancer are frequently exacerbated by depression (American Cancer Society, "Cancer Facts and Figures." 2010).

Cancer, perhaps the most dreaded diagnosis in our society, triggers a series of life-changing decisions that increase stress and vulnerability (Roesch et al, 2005). Patients may express feelings of uncertainty, loss of control, and even powerlessness. Disruptions in social relationships, emotional well-being, physical well-being, and role functions affect general quality of life. Chemotherapy, radiation, and surgical treatments can add to the psychological stress of cancer (American Cancer Society, "Cancer Facts and Figures," 2010). Also, medical treatments often disrupt the ability to attend to normal workplace activities as well as activities at home and in social environments (Franks & Roesch, 2006).

In the U.S., diabetes affects 25.8 million people among all ages, races, and ethnicities (CDC, "National Diabetes Fact Sheet," 2011) and is the seventh leading cause of death (DeCoster & Cummings, 2005). Research has shown that negative emotions such as fears, irritation and sadness are a common occurrence with diabetes (American Diabetes Association, 2011). Rates of depression have been found to be three times higher in people with diabetes than the general population. Major depression is diagnosed in one of every four patients with both types of diabetes (Antai-Otong, 2007). Frequently, co-occurring depression and diabetes is related to vascular complications which significantly increase the risk of coronary artery disease (CAD) and diabetes related death.

Mood disorders are the most common psychological disorder among patients with chronic kidney disease (CKD) including end stage renal disease (ESRD) (Christensen & Ehlers, 2002). According to the National Kidney Foundation (2011), 26 million people suffer from CKD. Physical symptoms of CKD worsen with co-occurring depression. Individuals with CKD and depression may experience an overlap of such symptoms (common to both illnesses) as fatigue, low energy, difficulty with concentration, lack of appetite, and insomnia. ESRD is a life-threatening and potentially disabling illness that affects 500,000 Americans (Khalil & Frazier, 2010). Some research shows that hospitalizations for individuals with co-occurring ESRD and depression are twice as high as for those without ESRD and may be attributed to an individual's non-compliance with his or her treatment plan (Christensen & Ehlers, 2002).

Non-compliance to treatment may be influenced by demographic factors (age, gender, educational level, and/or patient-doctor relationship) or psychosocial factors (depressive symptoms and/or social support) or the interaction of both (Khalil & Frazier, 2010). The management of ESRD can be quite stressful and quite possibly lead to an increase in depressive symptoms. A variety of stressors related to CKD include significant changes in lifestyle, familial roles, social identity, and personal control (Christensen & Ehlers, 2002). Depressive symptoms can affect morbidity, mortality, functional status and quality of life and can contribute to malnutrition or undernourishment because of decreased appetite (Khalil & Frazier, 2010). There is evidence to suggest that depression can be successfully treated with appropriate therapies (Christensen & Ehlers, 2002).

Chronic lung disease includes such illnesses as lung

cancer, chronic obstructive pulmonary disease (COPD) also known as emphysema and chronic bronchitis, and asthma. The CDC (2002) reports that a 2000 survey estimated that 24 million people presented with evidence of impaired lung functioning. In 2005, COPD was the fourth leading cause of death in the U.S. and, among cancer patients in 2007, lung cancer caused the most deaths (American Lung Association, 2011). Patients with COPD face declining pulmonary function, decreasing physical ability, and the loss of quality of life along with the possibilities of depression, anxiety, fatigue and fear (Wall, 2007). COPD also interferes with the ability to work and participate in personal care. People with COPD are at high risk for depression in that the likelihood of depression is 2.5 times greater for those with severe COPD than for those without (Nguyen & Carrieri-Kohlman, 2005). Compared to those with heart failure, arthritis, angina and diabetes, those with COPD were found to have worse psychological functioning.

Depressive and anxiety symptoms have been found in nearly half of COPD patients (Cully et al, 2006). Worsening depressive symptoms are associated with declining health-related quality of life, diminishing functional status, greater COPD symptoms, decreasing ability to cope, and failing treatments for COPD exacerbations (Nguyen & Carrieri-Kohlman, 2005). The mortality risk is three times greater for patients with depressive symptoms and COPD during hospitalization than for those without depression. Sadly, less than 25% of those with COPD and moderate-severe anxiety or depressive symptoms receive any treatment to address those symptoms (Kunik et al, 2008).

Statement of the Problem

Depression and co-occurring chronic physical illness is a serious issue for our society today and there is a need for greater concern regarding psychological interventions. Livneh and Antonak (2005) reported that roughly 54 million Americans, or 1 in 5, have some form of physical, sensory,

11

psychiatric, or cognitive disability that interferes with daily living. Depressive symptoms are common in older adults and are associated with disability and physical decline (Cho et al, 2010). Eight out of the ten most common causes of death are chronic illnesses often accompanied by depression and/or anxiety (Livneh & Antonak, 2005).

Diagnosis of a chronic illness often triggers a grief process related to the loss of a body part or function and includes feelings of bereavement and despair (Livneh & Antonak, 2005). Individuals are continually reminded of the permanency of their condition. Further, chronic illness may distort a person's body image and self-concept. Maladjustment is evidenced by feelings of depression and anxiety, chronic fatigue, psychogenic pain, cognitive dysfunction, and social withdrawal. Depression related to a chronic illness includes feelings of helplessness, hopelessness, distress, isolation, and despair. In addition, depression is a reflection of a person's acknowledgment of the magnitude of the illness, his or her realization that the condition is permanent, and understanding the future implications of the disease.

Effective coping, then, is a strategy needed by affected individuals to modify, diffuse, and/or decrease the effects of the stressors that come with a chronic illness diagnosis (Livneh & Antonak, 2005). Early screening and detection of depressive symptoms may play a role in developing psychological interventions that empower individuals with effective coping skills. Understanding potential risk factors for the development of depressive symptoms will provide the basis for clinicians to engage in early screening. One study found that a prior history of depression (not currently depressed) was associated with declining physical health over time (Cho et al., 2010). This is an important finding for primary care and specialty care settings, showing the need for careful screening for not only current depression but also for a history of depression even when patients seem to be in full remission.

Purpose of the Study

Research shows that individuals with a chronic physical illness struggle with symptoms of maladjustment, depression, and anxiety. The purpose of this study is to investigate the relationships among depression and chronic physical illness, screening for depression, risk factors for developing depression and potential psychological interventions. Three primary questions guided this study: 1) is there a positive relationship between symptoms of depression and chronic physical illness? 2) When is the best time to screen individuals with chronic physical illness for depression? 3) What are the primary risk factors for developing depressive symptoms among individuals with chronic physical illness and 4) what psychological interventions have been shown to reduce symptoms of depression while also reducing symptoms of chronic physical illness? These questions need to be answered because the results of this study can have an impact on how and which services are delivered by medical and mental health professionals while building a case for the

14

utilization of effective psychological interventions that could possibly lower the cost of healthcare in the United States.

Theoretical Framework

Depression is a significant public health problem, and the Medical Outcomes Study reports that the impairment and disability associated with depression is the same as that associated with cardiovascular disease and greater than other chronic physical illnesses such as hypertension, diabetes, and arthritis (Roberts, Kaplan, Shema & Strawbridge, 1997). . Studies show that the risk of developing depression increases with advancing age, and older adults are commonly diagnosed with depression or depressive symptoms. Perceived physical health, difficulties with ADL's and perceived mental health have all been found to be correlating risk factors for developing depression.

In 2003, the New Mexico Behavioral Risk Factor Surveillance System (BRFSS) survey found that most people needing treatment for depression did not receive treatment (Daniel, Honey, Landen & Marshall-Williams, 2005).   Barriers to treatment included stigmatization of depression, a lack of knowledge about depression, and inadequate insurance coverage.   Individuals were more likely to seek treatment from primary care physicians rather than psychiatrists, psychologists or social workers. As a result of this study, the U.S. Preventative Services Task Force (USPSTF) recommends that primary care settings ensure accurate diagnosis, effective treatment and follow up screening adults for depression. Early screening can increase the correct identification of depressed patients and treatment can decrease clinical morbidity.

Research Questions

This study intends to explore the following questions.   What relationship exists between chronic physical illness and symptoms of depression?   What methods are used to screen for depressive symptoms and when is the best time to conduct screenings? What risk factors exist that predict the development of depression or

16

depressive symptoms? And what psychological interventions affect symptoms of depression among individuals who have been diagnosed with or self-report at least one chronic illness? Is there a relationship between decreased symptoms of depression and decreased physical symptoms of chronic illness?

Importance of the Study

Research that focuses on answering these questions has great value for our country. Medical social workers who provide assistance through home care services can implement successful screenings and interventions while collaborating with primary care physicians. Chapman, Perry, and Strine (2005) agree that the burden of chronic disease would be greatly decreased by promoting mental health. Research that provides health professionals with tools for effective detection and intervention is priceless because of the greater quality of life those individuals with co-occurring mental and chronic physical illness will have.

Scope of the Study

To answer these research questions, the objectives of this study involve the review of scholarly journal articles related to the relationship between depression and chronic physical illness. In addition, the results of these previously conducted studies were analyzed for similarities and differences that may or may not support this study's hypotheses. Some journal articles contain data related to depression and chronic physical illness in general while other articles hold data related to depression and a specific chronic illness (such as arthritis, COPD, cancer, heart disease, hypertension, and diabetes). The literature includes studies conducted only in the United States, with adults diagnosed with depression and one or more of the top chronic physical illnesses. This study did not consider any articles that involved individuals with acute physical illnesses or any other mental illnesses.

Definitions

For the purposes of this study, significant terms are

18

defined as follows.

Chronic physical illness or chronic disease: a long-term
illness or disease than can be managed but not
cured (CMCD, 2011).

Depression: a mental illness diagnosed through the
demonstration of specific symptoms as determined
by the DSM-IV-TR (APA, 2000).

Depressive Symptoms: symptoms of a Major Depressive
Disorder listed in the DSM-IV-TR (APA, 2000).

Adults: any individual over eighteen years of age.

Summary and Organization of Remaining Chapters

Understanding the connection between depression
and chronic physical illness has importance because of the
need for both recognition of the prevalence of co-occurring
illnesses and of effective psychological interventions. The
recognition of such has the potential to affect the cost of
healthcare and change the way services are provided in
home health care and other medical professional facilities.
Perhaps even insurance companies such as Medicare and

Medicaid will recognize the benefit that psychological interventions provide in keeping physical health care costs down and, as a result, provide greater reimbursement for these services. This study builds this case through the discussion of a literature review, research methods and procedures, data analysis, research findings, limitations, and implications for further research.

Chapter Two: Literature Review

Depression Criteria

Mental health professionals use the Diagnostic and Statistical Manual of Mental Disorders, Fourth Edition-Text Revision (DSM-IV-TR) as their standard for diagnosing mental illness including depressive disorders. Medical professionals use the International Statistical Classification of Diseases, Ninth Revision Clinical Modification (ICD-9-CM) as their standard for coding both physical and mental illness for insurance reimbursement. On common ground, both classification systems seek to improve communication among clinicians, develop understanding of a multitude of disorders, and encourage effective treatment (Gruenberg, Goldstein, & Pincus, 2005). Since 1948, these two diagnostic manuals have seen several revisions in an attempt to keep up with each other and maintain similar criteria for diagnoses.

The DSM-IV-TR describes the diagnostic criteria for four depressive disorders: major depressive disorder single episode, major depressive disorder recurrent, dysthymic disorder, and depressive disorder-not otherwise specified (NOS) (APA, 2000). Most of the depression screens discussed in this paper reflect depressive symptoms consistent with major depressive disorder. To be diagnosed with major depressive disorder, an individual must meet three criteria. Criterion A states that there must be a single major depressive episode present.

To qualify for a major depressive episode, an individual must meet five criteria. First, criterion A says that, in a two-week period, five or more symptoms specified by the DSM-IV-TR must be present as a change from previous functioning and at least one of the symptoms needs to be either depressed mood or loss of interest or pleasure (APA, 2000). Those symptoms specified by the DSM-IV-TR include the following (either by self-report or by observation of others):

- Depressed mood most of the day nearly every day
- Decreased interest or pleasure in all or nearly all activities most of the day nearly every day

22

- Either weight loss or weight gain (within a month, change of more than 5% of body weight) or change in appetite nearly every day
- Changes in sleep patterns nearly every day (either lack of or excessive)
- Psychomotor agitation or retardation nearly every day that is both self-report and observed by others
- Loss of energy or increased fatigue nearly every day
- Feelings of excessive or inappropriate feelings of guilt and/or worthlessness nearly every day
- Decreased concentration or inability to make decisions nearly every day
- Recurrent thoughts of death, suicidal ideation without a plan, suicide attempt, or specific plan to commit suicide

Criterion B says that symptoms cannot meet criteria for a mixed episode, and criterion C states that symptoms must cause clinically significant distress or impairment of functioning in the occupational, social or other arenas. To meet criterion D, symptoms must not be attributable to the physiological effects of a general medical condition or substance and, to meet criterion E, they cannot be better explained by bereavement.

Assuming that an individual has met the criterion for a major depressive episode (criterion A of major depressive disorder), he or she, then, needs to meet criterion B which says that symptoms cannot be attributed to schizoaffective disorder or in conjunction with schizophrenia, schizophreniform disorder, delusional disorder, or psychotic disorder not otherwise specified (APA, 2000). Criterion C specifies that the individual being assessed cannot have experienced a manic, mixed or hypomanic episode. With all three criteria met, an individual can be diagnosed with a major depressive disorder single episode. If there have been two or more major depressive episodes, then the individual can be diagnosed with major depressive disorder recurrent.

In the ICD-9-CM manual, medical professionals have different diagnostic possibilities for depression than mental health professionals who rely upon the DSM-IV-TR. Coding in the ICD-9-CM for depressive disorders includes 296.2 (major depressive disorder, single episode), 296.3 (major depressive episode, recurrent episode), and 296.9 (other and unspecified episodic mood disorder) with the option to specify severity with a fifth digit ranging from 0 to 6: unspecified, mild, moderate, severe without psychotic behavior, severe with psychotic behavior, in partial or unspecified remission, and in full remission (Buck, 2009). Major depressive disorders either single or recurrent episode may include depressive psychosis, endogenous depression, involutional melancholia, manic-depressive psychosis or reaction-depressed type, monopolar depression, or psychotic depression but must exclude circular type, depression NOS, and reactive depression neurotic or psychotic. Options for 296.90 (unspecified episodic mood disorder) include affective psychosis NOS, melancholia NOS, and mood disorder NOS, while 296.99 (other specified episodic mood disorder) includes mood swings that rebound and are brief compensatory.

Medical professionals use the ICD-9-CM to code all mental disorders for purposes of insurance reimbursement and may use it to diagnose as well. According to the ICD-9-CM, psychosis is a "disturbance of great magnitude in which there is a personality disintegration and loss of contact with reality" (Buck, 2009). All mood disorders lie within the coding spectrum of psychoses. The ICD-9-CM does not provide any direction for medical professionals regarding symptoms of depression, so many rely upon their education and understanding of depression to form their diagnosis. Some may choose to utilize a depression screening tool to help them identify and diagnose depressive disorders.

Depression Screening

In 2004, Thomas and Brantley reported that primary care providers fail to identify and treat between 35% and 70% of patients with depressive disorders. Several tests have been developed to screen for depression and the lack of detection in primary care settings has created the need for more efficient and routine screening methods. The top criticisms that primary care providers cited regarding the use of screening tools include the amount of time needed for and difficulty of administration. Physicians have also stated that negative patient reactions and potential stigmatization of patients affect their reluctance to use current screening tools (Scogin & Shah, 2006).

Patients express concern related to the confidentiality of the screen as part of their hesitance to complete a depression screen while in their doctor's office (Scogin & Shah, 2006). Older women have described the General Health Questionnaire as stigmatizing, inappropriate and intrusive. Scogin & Shah (2006) believe, though, that adults may be less resistant than previously thought because of two studies that showed that 93.6% and 92% of participants viewed depression screens favorably. Research suggests that screening for depression, in addition to the provision of treatment and follow-up, improves the recognition of depression as well as treatment outcomes for adults in primary care settings. Therefore, the U.S. Preventative Services Task Force recommends that adults be screened in clinical practice where there is also a system in place for diagnosis,

27

treatment and follow-up.

It is possible that the lack of detection in the primary care setting comes from health care providers and patients' beliefs that depression is an expected side-effect of interpersonal loss, a decline in functioning and chronic medical illnesses that often come with aging (Brown & Shinka, 2005). Other potential obstacles in identifying depressive disorders in older adults in primary care include system delivery, clinician expertise, and patient characteristics. Time restraints and reimbursement restrictions are examples of system delivery barriers. Lack of knowledge regarding how depressive symptoms manifest and present differently between young and older adults can prove to be a significant problem for clinicians to overcome. Numerous patient characteristics that may impede the recognition of depression include a hesitancy to admit symptoms, social stigma, reporting somatic complaints rather than psychiatric complaints, a belief that depression is inevitable and a normal part of aging, and a preference to seek medical care instead of psychiatric care.

Identifying depression will help with the maintenance and improvement of the health and function of older adults (Friedman, Heisel, & Delaran, 2005) as well as aid in reducing the impact of a global health concern (Merz, Malcarne, Roesch, Riley & Sadler, 2011). Attempts to improve the identification of depression in older adults have been largely centered on the use of self-report questionnaires (Brown & Shinka, 2005). Many researchers have discussed some legitimate criticisms of self-report measures. Some scales assess somatic symptoms which could just as easily be the result of a physical disorder as of a mental disorder; this leads to an uncertainty that symptoms help discern the difference between mental health and mental illness (Wancata, Alexandrowicz, Marquart & Friedrich, 2006). Questions found in the self-report measures may be suitable for younger people but may cause difficulties for elderly people. Individuals with impaired cognitive functioning may find the complex response format confusing and be unable to successfully answer many of the questions.

Diagnostic interviews are considered by many to be the gold standard for identifying depression, but they are not suited for the primary care setting because the interviews are time-consuming and clinicians need screenings to be brief (Merz et al, 2011). Consequently, self-report questionnaires gained popularity because they can be administered and scored quickly. It cannot be assumed, however, that self-report measures always assess the construct they are supposed to for every individual, especially when diverse ethnic and language groups were not included in the standardization of those measures. Some of the more popular self-report questionnaires for depression screening include the Beck Depression Inventory II (BDI-II), the Center for Epidemiological Studies Depression Scale (CES-D), the Geriatric Depression Scale (GDS), and the Patient Health Questionnaire Nine Symptom Checklist (PHQ-9).

The BDI-II, revised in 1996 (Grothe, Dutton, Jones, Bodenlos, Ancona & Brantley, 2005), is a frequently used self-report questionnaire that was developed to 1) be more closely aligned with the diagnostic criteria of major depressive disorder (MDD) as presented in the DSM-IV-TR and 2) include atypical and severe depressive symptoms (Quilty, Zhang, & Bagby, 2010). Twenty-one items inquire about the frequency of symptom occurrence over a two-week time period. Participants rate frequency on a four-point Likert scale: 0 = not at all, 1 = several days, 2 = more than half of the days, and 3 = nearly every day. With a total possible score of 63 (Grothe et al, 2005), higher scores reflect a greater severity of depression (Quilty et al, 2010).

Beck recommended that clinicians use the total score on the BDI-II as a guide for depression severity in patients who were diagnosed with depression by way of the clinical interview (Quilty et al, 2010). When the BDI-II was factor analyzed, researchers found that the questionnaire items divided themselves into two or three symptom sets.

31

This raises questions about the overall usefulness and clinical meaning of a total score suggesting that subscale scores may be justified. The reason this is such an important question is because different populations may present with different factor structures of the BDI-II.

Previous research does show that the BDI-II has good psychometric properties, high internal consistency, good test-retest reliability, and good construct and concurrent validity (Grothe et al., 2005). A two-factor model (cognitive and somatic) has been proven valid for use among outpatient psychiatric care, primary care medical patients, inpatient geriatric patients, and college students. Three-factor models have demonstrated usefulness among psychiatric outpatient adolescents (cognitive, somatic, and guilt/punishment) and college students (negative attitude, performance difficulty, and somatic elements). Studies show moderately stable psychometric properties across groups; however, the majority of participants have been middle class Caucasian individuals.

Grothe et al. (2005) argue that there are racial differences in how individuals express depressive symptoms. They do not believe it can be assumed that the reliability and validity of the BDI-II will continue to be accurate for African Americans who often express more somatic symptoms and less typical symptoms of depression. In their study, Grothe et al. (2005) administered the BDI-II to 220 low-income medical outpatient African Americans, and they found strong evidence to support the reliability and validity of the BDI-II with this population. Though the BDI-II has been translated into Spanish, Wiebe and Penley (2005) at the time of their study reported that the Spanish version had not yet been pilot-tested and they could find little research regarding its psychometric properties and how it compared to the English version. Their study included 895 bilingual undergraduate students. Results showed both versions of the BDI-II to be reliable, internal consistency to be strong, and test-retest reliability to be acceptable.

The CES-D is a 20-item self-report questionnaire evaluating symptoms experienced over the previous week, and it has found the most use within the research field (Edwards, Cheavens, Heiy & Cukrowicz 2010). This measure, based on aspects of factor analytic and clinical studies, was created to measure depressive symptoms in the general population. The designers intended the CES-D to accomplish three things: represent numerous dimensions of depression, discourage response-bias (by way of reverse scored items), and assess positive affect. There is some debate that the CES-D may be too long of an assessment for use as a screening instrument in medical and rehabilitation settings (Martens et al., 2006). However, if it is used in primary care settings for the purpose of identifying depression, then knowing the impact of co-morbid chronic physical illness is needed as well (Thomas & Brantley, 2004).

Scores on the CES-D may be evaluated across four

components including depressed affect, positive affect, somatic and retarded activity, and interpersonal relationships. Replications of the four-component model have successfully occurred with urban residents, married men and women, primary care patients, university students, and both English and Spanish speaking individuals in psychiatric outpatient care (Edwards et al., 2010). It has also been supported among White, Black, Hispanic, and Mexican American adults. A four-factor model with one second-order factor found success in its use among samples of community living adults, adult women, and patients with rheumatoid arthritis. Some researchers discovered a valid three-factor structure (including the combination of somatic and depressed affect or the combination of depressed affect and interpersonal relationships) that worked well with ethnically diverse samples such as American Indian adolescents, adults, and elders. A five-factor structure has been proposed but has not received wide acceptance as a successful measure of depression.

Carlson et al. (2011) report that the CES-D works fairly well among numerous older adult populations to assess depression. Reverse-scored items like those in the CES-D use a structure that can be problematic for older participants for two reasons. First, respondents are forced to recognize the altering direction of the wording and secondly, they are required to utilize the opposite end of a rating scale in order to answer questions that are consistent with previous answers given. As a result, this format creates a potential methodologically induced bias. The confusion that this raises can lead individuals to provide responses that are directionally opposite to that which would be appropriate. Among older adults, the CES-D reverse-scored items have been reported to be less internally consistent and more weakly correlated with total scale scores than non-reversed items.

Some researchers state that, when studies like the CES-D use cutoff scores, they indicate adequacy in three ways: sensitivity, specificity, and negative predictive value (Martens et al., 2006). Sensitivity refers to the extent to which depressed individuals are identified based on that cutoff score. Specificity, on the other hand, is the degree to which non-depressed individuals are recognized based on the set cutoff score. The negative predictive value (NPV) is the proportion of individuals who are not depressed when their scores show they are not depressed. CES-D cutoff scores have been found to show poor positive predictive value (PPV), referring to the proportion of people who are actually depressed when the cutoff scores demonstrate they are depressed. Cutoff scores may result in an increased percentage of "false positive" results, meaning that individuals are identified as depressed but do not meet the diagnostic criteria for a major depressive disorder.

The full Geriatric Depression Scale (GDS) is a well-validated 30-item scale designed to help clinicians differentiate depression and dementia (Brown & Schinka, 2005) and is a popular screening tool used with the elderly

(Lopez, Quan, & Carvajal, 2010). The recommended GDS classification includes the following score ranges: 0-9 indicates normal mood, 10-19 indicates mild depression, and 20-30 indicates severe depression. It also includes an assessment of somatic symptoms which some criticize confuses a depressive diagnosis with physical illnesses common among the elderly (Friedman et al., 2005). An advantage of this screen is the forced yes or no format that requires little cognitive processing (Lopez et al., 2010). However, using this screen with cognitively impaired individuals is debatable because participants need to be able to recall emotional symptoms for the week prior to taking the test.

A shortened form of the GDS (15 item) was developed for use with people who express fatigue as a significant issue and for medical professionals who have to consider time constraints (Brown & Schinka, 2005). Depending upon the cut-off score used, this scale demonstrates adequate sensitivity and specificity as well as criterion validity in cognitively mixed populations of elder adults. Researchers, though, disagree with the reliability of the GDS to diagnose depression in people with dementia (Lopez et al., 2010). Poor memory can lead to guessing and may, consequently, lower internal consistency reliability and inter-item correlations. Older adults who have been administered the GDS-15 have expressed that the screening is acceptable and is not too stressful or difficult to complete (Scogin & Shah, 2006).

Used often in primary care and research settings, the PHQ-9 is a nine item screening tool that takes approximately five minutes for participants to complete and clinicians only one minute to score (Merz et al., 2011). These nine items match the diagnostic criteria (or symptoms) of Criterion A for major depressive episode as defined in the DSM-IV-TR (Cannon, Tiffany, Coon, Scholand, McMahon & Leppert, 2007). Participants report how often over a two week period they have experienced nine symptoms: anhedonia, depressed mood, sleep difficulties, fatigue, changes in appetite, feelings of worthlessness or guilt, difficulty concentrating, motor agitation, and suicidal ideation (Merz et al., 2011). Symptoms are rated on a four point Likert scale: 0 = not at all, 1 = several days, 2 = more than half of the days, and 3 = nearly everyday. The sums of scores range from 0-27 and a greater score means greater severity of depressive symptoms. It is recommended that a clinical cutoff score of 10 or higher be used to identify individuals who need further diagnostic evaluation to more accurately assess their level of depression.

Several medical professionals utilize the PHQ-9 eagerly because it is brief and demonstrates great psychometric properties (Merz et al., 2011). This tool has also been found to have good internal consistency, reliability and criterion validity. It proves to have good sensitivity and specificity values because of its ability to distinguish between depressed and non-depressed individuals. The PHQ-9 has been translated into many languages, showing that it can be widely accepted for cross-cultural use. Williams, Heinemann, Bode, Wilson, Fann, and Tate (2009) reported that this screening tool is preferred in spinal cord injury research and is also equally functional across gender.

One criticism of the PHQ-9 is that it does not include all of the DSM-IV-TR criteria for either major depressive episode or major depressive disorder (Cannon et al., 2007). This tool does not ask about criteria B (mixed episodes), D (symptoms cannot be due to substance abuse or general medical condition) or E (symptoms cannot be better accounted for by normal bereavement). An optional tenth question (though not used in scoring) is available on the screening tool and asks about major depressive episode criterion C: do symptoms cause clinically significant impairment? In order for a diagnosis of major depressive disorder to be given, the DSM-IV-TR requires that other conditions be ruled out (which the PHQ-9 does not evaluate) such as schizoaffective disorder, psychosis and manic, mixed and hypomanic episodes.

Regardless of which of the screening tools are used, the goal remains the same: to identify individuals who currently express symptoms of depression. Some research seeks to evaluate the usefulness of depression screening tools so that mental health and medical professionals can adequately identify depression diagnoses. Other research focuses on factors that may place individuals at risk for developing depression, factors that may increase depression and treatment factors that may decrease depressive symptoms. The following section of this study discusses the prevalence of depression among individuals with co-occurring chronic physical illnesses and potentially effective psychological interventions.

Literature Summaries

Depression and Chronic Illness. Depression has a significant impact on the physical state of those who have been diagnosed with chronic illness, and, conversely, chronic illness has a major influence on the severity of an individual's emotional state. Positive affect refers to the extent to which an individual feels enthusiastic, alert, and active (Hu & Gruber, 2008). A person with high positive affect will be pleasurably engaged, highly energetic and fully concentrated while someone with low positive affect will express sadness and lethargy. Negative affect involves subjective distress and less than pleasurable engagement. High negative affect is expressed in an individual as emotional pain and distress while low negative affect is expressed as calmness.

Studies suggest that older adults, who have a positive affect experience fewer chronic illness symptoms, less pain, and better quality of life while those with a negative affect will express increased symptoms, decreased functioning and poorer quality of life (Hu & Gruber, 2008). Hu and Gruber (2008) investigated the effects that positive and negative affect had on health functioning in terms of health-related quality of life, depressive symptoms, functioning and symptom distress.

43

They collected data from 153 adults aged 60 years and older who self-reported at least one of the following illnesses: arthritis, cardiovascular disease, COPD, or diabetes. Six measures were used to collect data including the Positive and Negative Affect Scale (PANAS), Symptom Distress Scale (SDS), Geriatric Depression Scale (GDS), Instrumental Activities of Daily Living Scale (IADLS), and the Medical Outcomes Study Short Form Health Survey (SF-36). This study found that Caucasians showed higher distress levels and depressive symptoms than did African Americans (Hu & Gruber, 2008). African Americans had a significantly higher positive affect than Caucasians and adults 80 years of age and older had a lower negative affect.

By the year 2030, the number of elderly adults is expected to double, and 70 million people will be 65 years of age or older (Zauszniewski & Bekhet, 2009). Depression and chronic illness will continue to rise as well. Some suggest that being female (along with functional impairment, poor health and perceived lack of social support) places a person at a higher risk of developing depressive symptoms. Zauszniewski and Bekhet (2009) completed a descriptive study to examine the reliability and validity of the Center for Epidemiological Studies Depression Scale (CES-D) and whether elderly women with chronic conditions could be diagnosed as depressed or not depressed based on the cut-off scores of 12 shortened measures.

This study evaluated 250 older women from northeast Ohio retirement communities (Zauszniewski & Bekhet, 2009). Measures used included the Older Adults Resources and Services Multidimensional Functional Assessment Questionnaire (OARS MFAQ) and the CES-D. The mean score on the CES-D was 7.24 (SD = 6.93) indicating that these women exhibited few depressive symptoms. However, using a cut-off score of 16, 8.4% of women with less than 3 chronic conditions, 10.3% with 3-4 chronic conditions, and 20.7% with five or more chronic conditions all showed clinically significant depressive symptoms.

Besides being at risk for developing depression, people with chronic conditions are also at risk for developing suicidal thoughts and behaviors (Hirsch, Duberstein, & Unützer, 2009). The Dynamic Model of Affect states that uncontrollable or unpredictable experiences such as chronic illness make it harder for people to tell the difference between the positive and negative factors associated with those experiences. Suicidal ideation may contribute even further to the difficulty older adults have in distinguishing between those factors. Hirsch et al (2009) intended, through their study, to assess subjective happiness, which they define as having a sense of subjective well-being along with increased positive affect and life satisfaction. They believe that, while it seems unlikely that someone who is depressed would express happiness, a few studies show that individuals can experience positive and negative emotions at the same

46

time.   The purpose of their study was to examine the effects of happiness on distress related to suicidal ideation among older adults with a chronic medical condition and co-occurring depressive symptoms.

In 18 primary care clinics across five states, 1,549 individuals 60 years of age and older participated in the study conducted by Hirsch et al. (2009). Measures used to collect data for this study included the Structured Clinical Interview for DSM-IV (SCID), screening questions for two anxiety disorders, Rand 12 Short Form (SF-12), NEO Personality Inventory-Revised (NEO-PI-R), Mini-Mental Status Exam (MMSE), and the Hopkins Symptoms Checklist (HSCL). Analyses of the data collected showed that there is a significant positive correlation between suicidal ideation and anxiety as well as mood disorder severity. Happiness was found to be negatively correlated with suicidal distress. Out of all participants, 258 (14%) reported they had been distressed by their suicidal ideation.   The distress associated with suicidal ideation appeared to increase as the number of chronic illnesses increased; however, it seems to be moderated by happiness.

Personality characteristics may also be moderators of the distress felt by people with chronic illnesses. Jerant, Chapman, Duberstein and Franks (2010) state research reveals that enhancing an individual's self-efficacy or confidence to engage in necessary behaviors to manage his or her illness will ultimately improve illness outcomes. The question they have, though, is what is moderating the effects of that research? Discovering these moderators can essentially lead to a greater understanding of who would be most likely to respond to treatment, thus increasing the efficiency of service delivery. Jerant intended to investigate whether Five Factor Model (FFM) personality traits (agreeableness, conscientiousness, extraversion, neuroticism, and openness) had an impact on the primary outcomes of self-rated health.

Adults (n=415) 40 years of age and older with at

least one chronic illness (arthritis, asthma, COPD, congestive heart failure, depression, or diabetes) were randomly selected from 12 university-affiliated primary care network offices in Northern California (Jerant et al., 2010). Measures used include the NEO Five Factor Inventory (NEO-FFI) and the SF-36. The sample was predominantly female (n=321) and the mean age was 60 (range 41-95). Most participants (n=245) reported two or more chronic illnesses while the others only reported one chronic illness. Unfortunately, Jerant was not able to find any significant relationships between the FFM personality factors and levels of distress as recorded on the participants' self-rated health outcomes.

Depressive disorders can also affect social functioning, especially if individuals begin to withdraw from the family and friends who care about them. Most often when depressive disorders are discussed, they are defined by the Diagnostic and Statistical Manual for Mental Disorders Fourth Edition Revised (DSM-IV-TR). Shen,

Findley, Banerjea and Sambamoorthi (2010) argue that there are individuals who do not meet the DSM-IV-TR criteria but still express depressive symptoms that affect chronic illness and functioning. The primary goal of the study conducted by Shen was to compare the rates of major depression and minor depression among female veterans with at least one of three chronic illnesses (heart disease, hypertension, or diabetes).

Data for the Shen et al. (2010) study was gathered from VA and Medicare claims of women veterans. Out of 49,516 women with diabetes, heart disease and/or hypertension, the final sample size n=13,430 also had co-occurring depressive symptoms. Forty percent of the final sample had major depression and sixty percent had minor depression; the most common form was Not Otherwise Specified (NOS). Women with diabetes or diabetes and hypertension had higher rates of Major Depressive Disorder (MDD) than those who had hypertension only. Adults 75 years of age and older were more likely to have

NOS or minor depression than those less than 50 years of age who were more likely to have MDD.

Some researchers believe that the focus of study should be on improving quality of life (which includes understanding the impact of major and minor depression) not on treatment and quantity of life (Chen, Baumgardner, & Rice, 2011). Self-assessments of health-related quality of life (HRQOL) are gaining popularity among researchers and medical professionals who want to track health status. Chen sought to evaluate the relationship of the number of chronic illnesses with HRQOL outcomes. Data was collected from the 2007 Behavioral Risk Factor Surveillance System via random telephone surveys. The outcomes of interest included four measures of HRQOL from the CDC's Healthy Days Core Module: general health, mental distress, physical distress, and activity limitations.

The researchers found that those people with 0-1 chronic illness had a higher prevalence of mental distress than physical distress (Chen et al., 2011). Those with two or more conditions had a higher rate of physical distress than mental distress. Individuals with three or more conditions were more likely to report a poor HRQOL than those who had 1-2 conditions. Subjects with cardiovascular disease or diabetes were seven to eight times more likely to report poor to fair health than those individuals without any chronic illness.

A twelve-year prospective study conducted by Karakus and Patton (2011) assumed that depression would affect the development of at least one of four chronic illnesses (arthritis, heart problems/stroke, diabetes and cancer). They further examined whether baseline depression affected the number of chronic illnesses reported among older adults. Researchers gathered data from the U.S. Health & Retirement Survey (HRS) which involved men and women born between 1931 and 1941 as well as their spouses or partners. After restricting participation to those individuals who, at baseline, did not report any of the four illnesses mentioned above, the sample size equaled 3,645 subjects.

The HRS consisted of such measures as demographics (age, gender, race, marital status, education, and income), the self-report of chronic illness, a depression index based on the CES-D, a gross motor index, BMI, and cigarette smoking (Karakus and Patton, 2011). The majority of participants were male, White/Caucasian, married, high school graduate or above, and had an income of $20,000 or less. At baseline, 5.2% (n=190) met criteria for depression, and, at the conclusion of the study, 45.4% developed arthritis, 19% heart problems, 13.9% diabetes, and 10.6% cancer. Depression, reportedly, increased the reporting of arthritis by 10%, heart problems by 8.8%, and diabetes by 5% (cancer reporting was not effected by depression). As a result of these findings, the researchers concluded that depression is significantly associated with three of the four chronic illnesses.

In primary care settings, many depressed patients walk in and out without their providers detecting the depression. One study assumes that controlling depression will provide patients with the ability to control other chronic conditions (Maradiegue & Khan, 2013). In order to reach this goal, patients must have adequate screening for depression and that screen should include the multiple factors that put patients at risk (red flags), a measurement tool like the PHQ-9, and at least two generations of family history of illness (Maradieque & Khan, 2013; De Cock, Emons, Nefs, Pop, & Pouwer, 2011). The medical records of 90 patients (18-67 years of age) at a Community Health Clinic (CHC) in Northern Virginia provided a convenience sample for data collection. The majority of participants were employed, women, married, with less than high school education, and originally from Central America.

The review of medical records revealed that 51 of the 90 patients were "screened" for depression: seven were actually diagnosed with depression and 44 were noted to have at least one red flag putting them at risk for depression (Maradiegue & Khan, 2013). Researchers discovered that the health care providers did not document the use of any depression screening tool. Those patients diagnosed with depression did receive treatment consisting of medication and psychotherapy. This study demonstrates what the researches discussed in their evaluation; many patients at risk for depression are walking out of their primary care settings unnoticed and untreated.

Depression and heart disease. Rates of depression among heart failure patients were estimated in 2009 to be at twenty-two percent (Paukert, LeMaire, & Cully, 2009). This is double the rates for depression in the general population. Paukert focused the study on factors associated with depression among older veterans with heart failure in order to improve not only the recognition of depression but also the treatments appropriate for individuals with these co-occurring disorders. The measures used in this study include the Geriatric Depression Scale (GDS), Geriatric Anxiety Inventory (GAI), Kansas City Cardiomyopathy Questionnaire (KCCQ), Heart Failure Illness Intrusiveness Rating Scale (HFIIRS), Brief-COPE, Multidimensional Health Locus of Control Scale Form C (MHLOCS-FC), Chronic Disease Self-Efficacy Scale (CDSS) and the Multidimensional Scale of Perceived Social Support (MSPSS).

Half of the sample (52) expressed significant levels of anxiety and/or depression (Paukert et al., 2009). Interestingly, 88% of those diagnosed as anxious were also depressed while only 44% of those diagnosed as depressed were also anxious. According to the Mini International Neuropsychiatric Inventory (MINI) 28 individuals met criteria for a diagnosis of MDD or dysthymia and 22 met criteria for a diagnosis of anxiety. For comparison purposes, the sample was split into depressed (n=48) and non-depressed (n=56) groups. Participants in the depressed group were found to be significantly more depressed (GDS), more anxious (GAI), more physically limited by heart failure (KCCQ), more intrusive (HFIIRS), more maladaptive in coping responses (Brief-COPE), more likely to attribute control to chance (MHLOCS-FC), and more likely to have lower self-efficacy than the non-depressed group.

Building on this, Cully, Graham, Stanley, Ferguson, Sharafkhaneh, Souchek & Kunik (2010) use the Paukert et al. (2009) study as a resource in seeking a greater understanding of how physical symptoms and emotions affect the quality of life of heart failure patients. In addition, they wanted to examine the relationship among disease severity, depression, anxiety and quality of life as well as discover more effective interventions (Cully et al., 2010). Underlying the focus of the study is the assumption that depression and anxiety potentially fuel the burden of physical illness as much as or even more than the physical illness by itself. The multitude of measures used to gather data for this study included the GDS, GAI, Mini-

International Neuropsychiatric Interview (MINI), the New York Heart Association Functional Classification, Relative Risk Score, and the KCCQ.

Through telephone screenings 96 participants age 60 and older diagnosed with heart failure as determined by the above mentioned measures were selected and assigned equally to two groups: with or without significant depression as determined by the above mentioned measures (Cully et al., 2010). With 99% of the sample size male, 74% Caucasian, 59.4% married, 59.3% carrying a high school education or higher, and 42% earning between $10,000 and $20,000 annually, the researchers found that depression is correlated with a reduction in quality of life for ambulatory heart failure patients. The depression group also showed greater impairment in physical abilities, heart failure symptom frequency, symptom burden, and social functioning. As a result, the researchers believe that there is potential for a holistic approach to intervention that utilizes physical health monitoring and disease self-management while increasing mental health treatment and decreasing mental health stigma.

Holistic intervention may prove to have critical importance because of increasing evidence that the following are risk factors for morbidity and/or mortality in patients with coronary heart disease (CHD): anxiety, depression, anger, social isolation, mental stress and other psychosocial problems (Day, Freedland & Carney, 2005). Some individuals seek mental health treatment on their own; however, the majority of folks with co-occurring CHD and depression do not. There is a question about why this is and to what patients attribute the cause of their illnesses to be. Day conducted a study to determine whether patients are more likely to attribute the cause of their heart disease to negative emotions than patients who are less anxious or less depressed.

Patients were recruited for this study from a nuclear cardiology exercise stress testing lab (Day et al., 2005). The researchers used the following measures: Beck

Depression Inventory (BDI), Beck Anxiety Inventory (BAI), and a questionnaire regarding patients' perceptions of the cause of their heart disease. Sixty-nine patients made up the final sample size with a mean age of 63 years (SD=10). Twenty-five percent (n=17) scored mildly depressed, and 17% (12) scored moderate-severely depressed. Among the top eleven attributed causes of heart disease, stress, sadness, and nervous tension were included. Those who reported at least one negative emotion as the cause of heart disease numbered 26 (or 38%).

In a related study, Kubzansky, Cole, Kawachi, Vokonas and Sparrow (2006) sought to observe how far the relationships between anger, anxiety and depression overlap in their impact on CHD. They hypothesized first that CHD would be strongly associated with shared distress among the emotions of anger, anxiety and depression and secondly that there may be some unique effects of each emotion. The mean age of the final sample size (n=1306) was 61 years (SD=8.3). In 1986, participants were administered the Minnesota Multiphasic Personality Inventory (MMPI-2). The results of the study supported the hypothesis that shared general distress is associated with a greater risk of CHD.

Besides negative emotions affecting CHD, perceived low social support is also believed to contribute to CHD by increasing the risk of mortality and morbidity (Lett et al., 2009). Social support can be viewed in two domains: network (which is the structure of social relationships) and functional (which is the actual support given through that structure). Lett et al. (2009) believe that depression and low social support may be more accurately described as indirect measures of negative affect or personality type. In their study, they aimed to assess the underlying dimensions of social support and depression as well as the relationship between social support and depression.

Individuals for this study were gathered from the Enhancing Recovery in Coronary Heart Disease (ENRICHD) clinical trial in which 2,481 patients from eight clinical centers participated (Lett et al., 2009). Those who met a modified diagnostic criteria for depression or low social support were eligible for this study (final sample size that completed all measures n=705). The researchers used the following measures: Depression Interview and Structured Hamilton (DISH), ENRICHD Social Support Inventory (ESSI), Interpersonal Support and Evaluation List Tangible Support Subscale (ISEL-T), Perceived Social Support Scale (PSSS), Social Networks Questionnaire (SNQ), and the BDI. The mean age of participants was 60 years (SD=13) with 39% (n=319) expressing depression only, 28% (n=198) low social support only and 27% (n=118) both depression and low social support.

Three years after heart transplant, patients were 26% at risk for developing major depressive disorder, 17% at risk for adjustment disorder with anxious mood, and 17% at risk for posttraumatic stress disorder (Rybarczyk et al., 2007). A study conducted by Rybarczyk aimed to look at the levels and factors associated with negative affect and depression. Heart transplant recipients were recruited from the Cardiac Transplant Research Database, a large prospective study of quality of life outcomes between five and 10 years after transplant. The final sample size was 370 adults at least 21 years of age.

Participants completed 12 self-report measures including the Cardiac Depression Scale (CDS), PANAS-X (expanded form), Sickness Impact Profile (SID), Social Support Index (SSI), and the Heart Transplant Symptom Checklist (HTSC) (Rybarczyk et al., 2007). The mean age of subjects at the time of transplant was 54.3 years (range 22 to 75) and 59 years at the time of study participation. The CDS was moderately correlated with negative affect score (PANAS-X). The mean score on the CDS was 79.0 (SD=25.0) indicating 19% showed clinically significant depression scores.

Depression and cancer. While the above research looked at the association between depression and negative affect, several cancer studies have looked at the association between depression and coping. Many cancer patients will experience changes to their psychological well-being because of the cancer diagnosis (Schlegel, Talley, Molix & Bettencourt, 2009). Several studies (assessing predominantly urban women) suggest that personal differences in coping significantly affect that well-being. Schlegel et al. (2009) wanted to discover whether geographic location (urban vs. rural) influenced the coping and depressive symptoms' association among women diagnosed with and treated for breast cancer.

Oncology nurses at nine radiation clinics in Missouri recruited 223 breast cancer patients (Schlegel et al., 2009). The mean age of participants was 59.19 (SD=12.72) with more than half diagnosed with early stages (0 or I) of breast cancer. Patients were measured at three different Waves (study entry, 3 months & 6 months) using three surveys: the COPE Scale, the CES-D, and a covariates survey. Patients showed higher levels of depressive symptoms at Wave 1 (M=13.41; SD=9.74) than at Wave 2

(M=11.45; SD=9.74) and Wave 3 (M=10.76; SD=9.87). No differences between urban and rural women were found. Physical health was positively associated with depressive symptoms at all three Waves.

Sleep quality for cancer patients may also be influenced by depression (Hoyt, Thomas, Epstein and Dirksen, 2009). Cancer studies have linked sleep problems with a poorer quality of life, fatigue, distress, and problems with the neuroendocrine and immune systems. Hoyt et al. (2009) conducted a study to assess whether or not coping and depressive symptoms influence sleep quality among male cancer patients. In a southwestern U.S. metropolitan area, 55 men who had been treated for cancer were recruited from a Veterans hospital's outpatient oncology clinic for this study.

Participants completed questionnaires at study entry (T1) and again six months later (T2) (Hoyt et al., 2009). The measures used for this study included the Insomnia Severity Index (ISI), Brief-COPE, Emotional Approach

Coping Scale (EACS), an abbreviated CES-D (10-items), and the Impact of Events Scale-Intrusion subscale (IES-I). The mean age of subjects was 68.7 (SD=10.6) and 76% of the sample reported later stages of cancer (III & IV). Depressive symptoms above the clinical cutoff (Score ≥ 10) were expressed by 59.3% of men in this study, and the mean score for depression was 10.61 (SD=4.15). Hoyt et al. (2009) concluded that depressive symptoms are related to the interference of sleep as well as the severity of sleep difficulties for men who have cancer.

Lung cancer patients may be at risk for greater distress than those with other cancer diagnoses (Walker, Zona, & Fisher, 2006). Distress, however, may also be related to social support and a helpless/hopeless coping style. Some coping styles have been found to have an association with less hope, greater depression, and decreased survival rate. Walker decided to study the depressive symptoms of patients with new diagnoses of lung cancer and their coping styles while also looking at their social support systems. They proposed five hypotheses: a) action-oriented coping style that seeks social support will be negatively associated with depression, b) denial and disengagement coping style will be positively associated with depression, c) directive support will be associated with more severe depressive symptoms, d) non-directive support will be associated with less severe depressive symptoms, and e) social support would be related to coping style, while directive and non-directive social support would be associated in different ways with coping style.

Participants (n=119) who had been through a surgical resection for stage I or II small cell lung cancer were recruited from two cancer centers in Washington State (Walker et al., 2006). Written questionnaires were given to subjects, and they also went through an oral interview which included the completion of social support, coping, and depression measures. Measures included the Eastern Cooperative Oncology Group, COPE, SSI, and the

BDI. Oral interviews (either face to face or via telephone) were conducted at study entry (baseline) and follow up at 3, 6, 12, 24, and 36 months later.

At baseline, depressive symptoms were significantly associated with depressive symptoms at later times while social support at baseline was significantly correlated with depressive symptoms over time (Walker et al., 2006). The mean age of participants was 59.1 years (SD=10.0) with greater than half being female, married or living together and educated at a high school level or less. Regarding depression (BDI) at baseline, the mean score was 11.5 (SD=8.3) and regarding social support (SSI), the mean score was 4.01 (SD=0.72). The Adaptive coping mean score at baseline was 2.63 (SD=0.60) while the less-adaptive coping mean score was 1.74 (SD=0.52). The mean depression score was above the typical screening cutoffs; 28.7% of participants had a score at or above 16, indicating clinically significant depression. Additionally, depression scores among lung cancer participants were found to be negatively associated with age and positively associated with less adaptive coping as well as directive support.

As research has shown, cancer patients do have higher rates of psychological distress and lower quality of life than those without cancer (Pudrovska, 2010). Asking cancer patients if they are experiencing more years of distress or if they are living with a greater quality of life is important to mental health professionals and researchers alike. Pudrovska (2010) believed that not only were there differences in the experiences of patients with cancer over time, but there were also differences among men and women in their struggles with cancer. She operated her study under the theory that psychological adaptation to cancer depends upon the meanings and ideals associated with gender roles either through the cost of caring or the cost of dominance.

The cost of caring is tied to the traditional female role; beliefs that women possess the characteristics of nurturance, compassion and caring and they attend to the needs of others only to neglect their own (Pudrovska, 2010). Opposing this is the cost of dominance which is connected to the social-constructionist gender framework; beliefs that men represent authority, power and tradition as well as independence, competitiveness, dominance and control (including their emotions). For women, the cost of caring may increase their vulnerability to stressors because they assume more care giving and family responsibilities. Men, on the other hand, may be more depressed by cancer because it is more of a threat to their identity and they may possess fewer effective coping skills and resources to adjust to dependence, lack of control, and vulnerability that comes with the diagnosis and treatment of a chronic disease like cancer.

Pudrovska (2010) collected data from the Wisconsin Longitudinal Study, which consisted of a random sample of men and women who graduated high school in 1957 along with a random sample of their siblings. Participants (mostly

Caucasian) were interviewed on four occasions: 1957 (age 17 or 18 years), 1975 (age 36 years), 1993 (age 53 or 54 years) and 2004 (age 64 or 65 years). For the purpose of Pudrovska's study, only the interviews from 1993-1994 (T1) and 2004-2005 (T2) were used. In 1993-1994, subjects participated in a one-hour telephone interview and completed a self-administered questionnaire through the mail.

Eleven years later, subjects completed a second one-hour telephone interview and a 48-page survey through the mail. The focus of study for Pudrovska (2010) was on those participants (n=8,054) who completed all measures at both data collection times (3,565 men and 4,398 women). Six measures were used in this study: CES-D, physical characteristics (including comorbidities and symptoms), sexual activity, masculinity beliefs, sociodemographics, and control variables. Those who did not have a diagnosis of cancer at T1 but did so at T2 reported significantly more depressive symptoms than

71

those without cancer. Cancer survivors who were diagnosed with cancer both at T1 and T2 showed higher levels of distress than those without cancer.

Compared to patients without cancer, patients with cancer at T1 expressed 1.18 additional days per week of depressive symptoms while patients with cancer at T2 showed 1.35 additional days per week of depressive symptoms (Pudrovska, 2010). Individuals diagnosed between T1 and T2 reported more depressive symptoms than those without cancer. Men who had cancer at both T1 and T2 expressed significantly more depressive symptoms than the women who had cancer at both T1 and T2 (1.5 more days per week). Between T1 and T2, the men diagnosed with cancer showed one more day per week of depressive symptoms than women who were diagnosed between T1 and T2. Lastly, men with a cancer diagnosis did report higher distress levels than men without cancer while women did not show any differences in distress between those with cancer and those without cancer.

Else-Quest, LoConte, Shiller and Hyde (2009) believed that distress among cancer patients may be linked to self-blame, perceived stigma, and adjustment. Their primary hypothesis states that self-blame will mediate the link from perceived stigma to poor adjustment. In addition, they hypothesized that characterological self-blame is related to poorer psychological adjustment which includes incidents of higher rates of depression. Researchers recruited 172 cancer patients between 35 and 92 years of age (96 with non-small cell lung cancer, 30 with breast cancer, and 46 with prostate cancer) from the University of Wisconsin Comprehensive Cancer Clinic, William S. Middleton Memorial VA Hospital oncology clinic, and the University of Wisconsin Health Oncology clinic.

Only patients who were diagnosed with stage IV metastatic cancer were included in this study (Else-Quest et al., 2009). Among participants, 93.6% identified themselves as White (non-Hispanic), 66.8% as married or partnered, 91.2% as high school educated or above, and

63.3% as having an annual household income of $30,000 or greater. A questionnaire packet was mailed to subjects in order to assess their perceived stigma, self-blame, self-esteem, anxiety, anger, depressed affect and causal attributions. In this packet, the following measures were included: the State Shame and Guilt Scale (SSGS), Rosenberg's Inventory, the Spielberger State Trait Anxiety Inventory – state anxiety subscale, the Spielberger State Trait Anger Inventory, the CES-D, and an open-ended question regarding causal attribution.

A score of 16 or greater on the CES-D indicated depression and 20.6% of participants scored high enough to be diagnosed with depression (Else-Quest et al., 2009). In reviewing all of the data and in relation to the researchers hypotheses, they found that perceived stigma, though negatively associated with self-esteem, was positively associated with self-blame, anxiety, anger and depressed affect. Self-blame, negatively correlated with self-esteem but positively correlated with anxiety, anger

74

and depressed affect. Therefore, perceived stigma and self-blame are significant predictors of depression in patients with cancer. Interestingly, 72 patients (42%) who reported an internal causal attribution (meaning they blame themselves for their illness) demonstrated higher anxiety, anger, and depression.

Depression is seen by Kirkova et al. (2010) as a symptom of distress, and distress is associated with a poorer quality of life. The National Comprehensive Cancer Network recommends that cancer patients in an outpatient setting should be screened for overall distress (spiritual, physical, emotional, and family problems) using the Distress Thermometer. Kirkova examined the relationship of distress measured by a single question (whether or not it is bothersome) with self-assessed symptom severity using a categorical scale measure (mild, moderate, or severe). They also wanted to determine whether symptom prevalence (distress) was affected by demographics.

Referred by an attending physician and/or

continuing care, 181 patients ages 51 to 77 were assessed at their initial consultation by a palliative medicine program (Kirkova et al., 2010). Participants answered a 48-item checklist by categorically grading symptoms and the Cochran-Armitage trend test was used to determine whether distress increases with greater symptom severity. The study showed that greater severity was indeed associated with greater distress for most symptoms. More than 50% of subjects had clinically important symptoms they rated as distressful. Those with the worst performance status scores (3-4) exhibited more clinically important depression; 64 individuals (35%) identified a prevalence of depression and, of them, 34 (53%) expressed their depression as distressful. Females reported a higher prevalence of distress over the symptom of depression than males.

Rabkin et al. (2009) also theorized that depression is associated with greater distress in patients diagnosed with late stage cancer. However, these researchers asked different questions than did Kirkova et al. (2010) such as: 1) does depression occur as a new onset when death is imminent, 2) do mood levels change over time, and 3) are there any factors that either predispose a patient to or protect from the development of depression (Rabkin, McElhiney, Moran, Acree & Folkman, 2009)? This study recruited 58 late stage cancer patients with a life expectancy of 6 to 12 months and 58 caregivers. Through a convenience sample from the Oncology Service of New York Presbyterian Hospital, the UCSF Breast Cancer Clinic, a home care service of a community hospital, and an oncology service at a San Francisco VA hospital, the researchers selected their subjects. Data collection occurred at one-month intervals until participants' deaths, which equated to two to four in-person interviews per participant.

The measures used to collect data for this study include the MMSE, PHQ-9, Holland Systems of Beliefs Inventory, PANAS shortened version, Spielberger State

Trait Anxiety Inventory, and Visual Analogue Scales (Rabkin et al., 2009). Though the researchers evaluated demographics (marital status, gender, education, income and race), they only disclosed detailed information on race: 38% (n=22) identified as Black, 46.5% (n=27) identified as Caucasian and 15.5% (n=9) identified as other races. Mean education for the New York group (n=35) and the San Francisco group (n=23) differed significantly: 14.2 years (New York) versus 16.1 years (San Francisco). Related to income (51 of 58 participants disclosing), the researchers divided participants into two groups: those above a median income of $25,000 (n=27 or 47%) and those below a median income of $25,000 (n=24 or 41%).

At baseline data collection, 32% of patients (n=19) stated they had been depressed in the past and 23% of patients (n=13) reported receiving treatment for depression at the beginning of the study (Rabkin et al., 2009). Further analysis of the data showed that 3% of patients (n=2) expressed depression at all interviews and 14% of patients (n=8) did not exhibit any depression at baseline but at a later interview scored high enough to be diagnosed with depression. In a substudy, 24 patients (41%) engaged in 4 interviews which allowed the researchers to evaluate patterns of change as death became imminent. At baseline, one patient (4%) expressed depression; three months before death, no patients expressed depression; two months before death, two patients (8%) exhibited major depressive disorder; and, at the last visit before death, seven patients (29%) exhibited major depressive disorder. Of these 24 patients, four (17%) developed a new onset of depression; six patients (18%) of the 34 who did not engage in four interviews also developed a new onset of depression. Interestingly, onset diagnosis for seven (70%) of these ten patients (17% of total sample size N=58) with new diagnosis of depression occurred at the last visit before death.

Visual Analogue Scales employed a 10-point rating system where a response of 1 = "absent or not at all" and

10 = "always or nearly always" (Rabkin et al., 2009). Researchers asked patients to rate several of the same items included in the other studies in an effort to discover what factors may be contributing to or protecting from depression. They found that patients with stronger spiritual beliefs reported symptoms of anxiety less, expressed more hopefulness, exhibited a greater positive mood and experienced better overall satisfaction of life. In addition, patients identifying with a positive mood noted a positive correlation with spiritual beliefs, hope, pleasure, desire to live and overall satisfaction with life as well as an inverse relationship with depression, distress and anxiety.

A larger study conducted by Lichtenthal et al. (2009) investigated the rate of development of mental disorders (including depression) and distress as death closes in on patients diagnosed with advanced-stage cancer. The researchers hypothesized that the prevalence of psychiatric disorders (including depression) increases with impending death. Participants (N = 289) ages 48to 72 with advanced-stage cancer were recruited from a Coping with Cancer study that focused on the incidence of mental illness and the utilization of mental health services. Between August 1, 2002, and May 25, 2007, subjects from the Yale Center, the VA Connecticut Healthcare System, comprehensive cancer clinics in Connecticut, the Memorial Sloan-Kettering Cancer Center in New York, and the Parkland Hospital Palliative Care Service in Texas completed a 45-minute interview.

Criteria to participate in this study included the following: have a diagnosis of advanced-stage cancer from one of the above participating sites, be age 20 years or older, have an identified unpaid caregiver, speak English or Spanish, be able to tolerate the full interview, and not have dementia or delirium (Lichtenthal et al., 2009). To collect data, the researchers used demographic information, the Zubrod Performance Scale, the Karnofsky Performance Status Scale, the Charlson Comorbidity Index, the McGill Quality of Life Questionnaire, the Inventory of Complicated

Grief-Revised, self-reported terminal illness acknowledgement, the NIA/Fetzer Multidimensional Measure of Religiousness/Spirituality for Use in Health Research, and the existential subscale of the McGill Quality of Life Questionnaire. The SCID-I and the Endicott symptom substitution method were used to assess participants for major depressive disorder, generalized anxiety disorder, panic disorder, and/or post traumatic distress disorder while the Yale Evaluation of Suicidality Scale (first two items) was used to assess severity of suicidal risk. Assessment of the majority of participants occurred within six months of death.

Demographic information revealed that 63% of participants (n=182) identified as White, 18% (n=52) as Black, 17% (n=48) as Hispanic, 1% (n=3) as Asian, and 1% (n=2) as other races (Lichtenthal et al., 2009). Across gender, 56% (n=160) men and 44% (n=127) women participated in this study. The mean education level of subjects was reported as 12.4 years with a standard deviation of 4.1 years. Married participants made up 55% (n=158) of the sample size. The researchers found that 30 (10.8%) participants met eligibility for at least one of the four mental disorders (mentioned earlier as being assessed by the SCID-I) at study entry. Of these 30 participants, 14 (47%) met criteria for a diagnosis of depression. Incredibly, further analysis of the data revealed that the prevalence of mental illness did not increase or decrease as patients neared death.

Depression, diabetes, and chronic kidney disease. Distress among individuals with diabetes may have a significant impact on health behaviors including control of blood-sugar levels. In their longitudinal study, Chiu, Wray, Beverly and Dominic (2010) aimed to examine the relationship between symptoms of depression and control of blood-sugar levels of middle-aged and older adults diagnosed with Type 2 diabetes. They also sought to identify the strength of health behaviors that may explain the connection between these two variables. The hypotheses of the Chiu et al. (2010) study state that 1) symptoms of depression evaluated by the CES-D will be associated with coexisting and long-term health behaviors and 2) that association will be responsible for a significant portion of the link between symptoms of depression and control of blood-sugar levels.

Researchers gathered data from 998 adults (51 years of age and older) who self-reported a diagnosis of Type 2 diabetes (Chiu et al., 2010). These participants also expressed valid HbA1c levels in a 2003 mailed survey specific to diabetes. Two measures were used to assess depressive symptoms: the CES-D and the Composite International Diagnostic Interview – Short Form (CIDI-SF). Nearly 75% of participants reported at least three symptoms of depression at baseline, which categorizes them as moderately to severely depressed. They also showed significant lower baseline and follow up health behaviors.

However, these health behaviors, though significant,

did not completely explain the link between symptoms of depression and control of blood sugar levels (Chiu et al., 2010). Other factors that may have affected this link include anti-depressant therapy (as some medications can have a positive side-effect of lowering blood-sugar levels) or biological factors such as endocrinological processes, hypercortisolism or cortisol. Low levels of depression were found to be associated with non-compliance to treatment plans for diabetes care. Those non-compliant health behaviors include infrequent exercise, unhealthy diet, and smoking. Lifestyle behaviors despite proving to be reasonable factors in the link between depression and higher HbA1c levels may not be the only explanation for the depression-hyperglycemia relationship.

Similar to the study conducted by Chiu et al. (2010), Daly, Trivedi, Raskin & Grannemann (2007) also wanted to evaluate the relationship between glycemic control and depression. The aim of their study had three parts. The first was to examine the screening process that combines

85

two instruments designed to assess for major depressive disorder as well as the severity of symptoms. The second was to evaluate the prevalence of depression in the diabetic outpatient population. The last was to assess whether there was a significant difference between those with depression and those without depression in the control of blood sugar levels.

Consenting adults aged eighteen years and older from a diabetic outpatient clinic were recruited for participation in this study (Daly et al., 2007). The PHQ-2 and the Quick Inventory of Depressive Symptomatology (QIDS-SR) were administered to 89 adults. Using a cutoff score of 3 or greater, 37.1% of adults screened exhibited evidence of major depressive disorder. In addition, 27% demonstrated depressive symptoms that were not severe enough for a diagnosis of major depressive disorder.

Individuals with comorbid symptoms of major depressive disorder and diabetes in several studies have reported a decreased health-related quality of life.

Kaholokula, Haynes, Grandinett and Chang (2006) state that, compared with Caucasians, persons in the U.S. with Native Hawaiian, Japanese, and/or Filipino ancestry are twice as likely as a group to have Type 2 diabetes. The prevalence of depression among these individuals is 31.7% compared to 10% in the general population. The goal of this study was to review the extent to which there is a correlation between symptoms of depression and health-related quality of life across ethnic groups. It was a community based sample of individuals who had been diagnosed with Type 2 diabetes.

To participate in this study, individuals needed to be eighteen years of age or older, a resident of North Kohala, and if female, not pregnant (Kaholokula et al., 2006). The ethnic groups represented in this study include Native Hawaiians, Filipinos, Japanese, and those of mixed ethnic ancestry; a total of 179 people participated. Five measures were used to assess demographics (Personal History Form), glycemic status (HbA1c), depression (CES-D), health related quality of life (SF-36 Health Survey), and social support (Lubben Social Network 6-item subscale). No difference was found on the CES-D depression scores among the groups.

The researchers did find a significant negative association between the CES-D depression scores and the SF-36 subscales of emotional functioning, social functioning and physical functioning (Kaholokula et al., 2006). Native Hawaiians and Filipinos demonstrated a significant negative association between CES-D depression scores and the SF-36 subscales of bodily pain, general health, vitality, and physical functioning. In addition, Filipinos showed a significant negative association between CES-D depression scores and the SF-36 subscale of health transition. Among the Japanese, there were no significant associations between CES-D and SF-36. Interestingly, all four groups scored low on the CES-D. Japanese participants showed fewer depressive symptoms and Filipino participants demonstrated more depressive symptoms. Overall, those individuals who expressed more symptoms of depression also showed a significant decrease in physical functioning, general health perception and progression of disease as well as more severe and limiting body pain, less energy, and more emotional problems that affect work and other activities of daily living.

Individuals with increased depressive symptoms and a lack of social support may experience a decrease in healthy behaviors needed to successfully manage diabetes. Sacco and Yanover (2006) conducted a study to evaluate the following three theoretical concepts: 1) low social support increases depressive symptoms which in turn increase symptoms of diabetes, 2) diabetes symptoms increase symptoms of depression which then decreases social support, and 3) diabetes symptoms decrease social support which as a result increases symptoms of depression. From the University of South Florida Diabetes Center, 86 individuals participated in this study. The PHQ-9 was used to assess symptoms of depression while the

Global Support subscale of the Michigan Diabetes Research and Training Center Diabetes Care Profile was used to assess social support. Researchers found that depressive symptoms did play a role in the impact of social support on the medical symptoms of diabetes. In the reverse, depressive symptoms also mediate the effects of diabetes symptoms on social support.

Hoth, Christensen, Ehlers, Raichle and Lawton (2007) take the concept of social support and depressive symptoms a step further in their research related to chronic kidney disease (CKD) and the personality trait of agreeableness, which refers to the ability to be sympathetic toward others, to trust others' motives, and to be cooperative. The researchers' goal was to review the hypothesis that the correlation between symptoms of depression and social support varies among patients with CKD because of individual differences in agreeableness. They predicted that, for individuals high in agreeableness, greater social support would be correlated with fewer

90

symptoms of depression over time while, for those who scored low in agreeableness, social support would have minimal impact on symptoms of depression.

To be eligible for this study, participants needed to speak English, have a creatinine level over 3.0 mg/dL (indicating moderate impairment in kidney functioning), and be eighteen years of age or older without severe cognitive impairment (Hoth et al., 2007). A total of 59 people completed the BDI to assess depression, the Social Provisions Scale to assess social support, and the NEO-Five Factor Inventory to assess the personality trait of agreeableness. Results revealed that individual differences in agreeableness and social support were correlated with symptoms of depression for those with comorbid chronic kidney disease. For those who scored high in agreeableness, having greater social support correlated with a decrease in symptoms of depression over an 18 month period. As predicted, those who scored low in agreeableness, social support had very little impact on

91

symptoms of depression.

From a different angle, Kellerman, Christensen, Baldwin and Lawton (2010) examined the impact symptoms of depression had on mortality in CKD patients during a 7-year period. Again, participants had to be English speaking, eighteen years of age or older with no severe cognitive impairment, have a progressive form of renal disease and a creatinine level greater than 2.5 mg/dL. The measures that the 359 subjects completed included the BDI to assess depression as well as a demographic and clinical variable questionnaire. At follow-up, 216 participants were reported deceased and the causes of death were numerous. The researchers did find that total depression scores and non-somatic depressive symptom scores were significantly correlated with a higher mortality risk. More than half of the sample (54%) scored greater than 10 on the BDI indicating they were experiencing at least mild depressive symptoms.

Depression and arthritis. Individuals with arthritis

experience significant pain, and symptoms of depression could have a significant impact on those levels of pain. Zautra et al. (2007) developed three hypotheses concerning arthritis and depression: 1) Participants who have a history of multiple episodes (2 or more) of depression will be associated with greater arthritis pain, 2) participants who have a history of multiple episodes of depression will demonstrate greater perceived stress and lesser positive affect than those with no or only one episode of depression while undergoing lab induced stressors, and 3) participants who have a history of multiple episodes of depression will report higher levels of stress-reactive pain than those with no or only one episode of depression.

The only requirement to participate in this study involved written confirmation of rheumatoid arthritis from a rheumatologist (Zautra et al., 2007). Four assessments were conducted with 138 participants: baseline, after each stress induction activity (there were 2), and after recovery.

Measures used included the SCID to assess depression, two measures of pain, a self-report of current symptoms of depression, the Hamilton Depression Inventory, the Positive and Negative Affect Schedule, ratings of body pain and nerve pain, and physician assessments of joints for swelling and tenderness. Participants were divided into three groups: no depression, one episode of depression, and 2 or more episodes of depression.

Half of the participants were asked to come to a lab session in which stress was induced via two methods: a standard speech task and a discussion of an interpersonal conflict (Zautra et al., 2007). Regarding hypothesis 1, results showed that those individuals with multiple episodes of depression reported more pain than those who had no or only one episode of depression. For hypothesis 2, perceived stress was significantly higher for individuals with multiple episodes of depression. Hypothesis 3 was also supported in that individuals with multiple episodes of depression demonstrated greater pain with elevated stress levels. The researchers did explore other possible relationships such as the interaction effects between current symptoms of depression and reports of stress predicted pain but did not find a significant correlation.

Factors such as inadequate social support, decreased health and functioning, lack of psychological mastery, and the perceived impact of and inability to cope with rheumatoid arthritis may be associated with psychosocial risk for increased symptoms of depression (Morris, Yelin, Wong & Katz, 2008). Over an eight year period, Morris intended to recognize patterns of psychosocial risk in people diagnosed with rheumatoid arthritis. They looked at not only depressive symptoms but also at limitations in basic functioning, yearly number of physician visits, and pain perceptions. The researchers hypothesized that inadequate psychosocial resources would place people with rheumatoid arthritis at higher risk for poor long-term effects such as greater depressive symptoms, increased utilization of medical services, greater pain perceptions, and increased limitations on physical functioning.

This study recruited participants from the University of California San Francisco (UCSF) Rheumatoid Arthritis (RA) Panel Study of 1995 (Morris et al., 2008). All aspects of the study were completed by 344 participants over an eight-year period. Measures completed by participants included demographics, disease related factors, a 7-item scale from the UCSF RA Panel Study to assess perceived ability to cope with rheumatoid arthritis, the Satisfaction with Abilities and Well-Being Scale (SAWS) to assess perceived impact of rheumatoid arthritis and satisfaction with health functioning, the Berkmar Social Network Index to assess social support, a 7-item scale to assess psychological mastery, the GDS to assess depressive symptoms, the Health Assessment Questionnaire (HAS) to assess limitations on basic functioning, and 2 self-report rating scales of pain and average number of physician visits. A score of 7 or above on the GDS indicates depression, and 9.3% of the sample scored in this manner at baseline.

At baseline, 133 participants scored high risk, 192 scored moderate risk, and 236 scored low risk for poor long-term outcomes (Morris et al., 2008). The researchers discovered that these patterns of psychosocial risk were distinctively correlated with outcomes assessed yearly for eight years and especially on depressive symptoms as well as functional limitations due to rheumatoid arthritis. As a result, well-being and quality of life may be greatly affected. Cognitive Behavioral (CB) treatment is recommended by the researchers with an emphasis on coping skills and examining social support systems.

Depression and chronic lung disease. CB treatment may be helpful for lowering depressive symptoms in people diagnosed with Chronic Obstructive Pulmonary Disease (COPD). Kunik et al. (2008) set two objectives for their study: to evaluate the impact of CB group treatment and COPD education on 1) general and disease specific quality of life and 2) symptoms of depression and anxiety, six-minute walk distance, and the use of health related services. They hypothesized that CB group treatment would have a greater impact than COPD education. Individuals were included in the study if they had a diagnosis of COPD, moderate anxiety and/or depression, and received some form of treatment by a primary care physician or pulmonologist.

Depression was assessed with the BDI (a score of 14 or more indicated at least mild depression) and anxiety was assessed with the BAI (a score of 16 or more indicated at least moderate anxiety) (Kunik et al., 2008). CB group treatment consisted of eight one-hour sessions of interventions addressing both anxiety and depression. COPD education consisted of eight one-hour sessions: 45 minutes of lecture and 15 minutes of discussion. Participants completed assessments at weeks 4 and 8 as well as months 4, 8 and 12. Groups were randomized: 118 into CB group treatment and 120 into COPD education. Results showed significant improvement in BDI and BAI scores. However, differences were not seen between the two groups. Both CB group treatment and COPD education improved six-minute walking distance, symptoms of anxiety and depression, and quality of life significantly; in addition, improvements were sustained for the next 44 weeks.

Dyspnea management (DM) is yet another treatment studied by Nguyen and Carrieri-Kohlman (2005) for its impact on symptoms of depression. To be included in the study, individuals had to be at least 40 years old, have a confirmed diagnosis of moderate to severe COPD that had been clinically stable for one year or more, have hadno previous involvement in a formal exercise program or pulmonary rehabilitation during the past year, and have had no other active symptomatic illnesses. One hundred participants were recruited through ads and referrals and randomized to one of three treatment groups. Those groups included a) DM only, b) DM plus four supervised exercise sessions, or c) DM plus 24 supervised exercise sessions.

DM consisted of three parts: individualized education and demonstrations of how to self-manage dyspnea, home-based walking prescription, and self-monitored exercise programs (using a pedometer and a log) (Nguyen & Carrieri-Kohlman, 2005). Exercise sessions were nurse-supervised and on a treadmill. Participants completed the CES-D to assess depression (with a cutoff of 16 indicating high risk for depression), the Chronic Respiratory Questionnaire (CRQ) to assess dyspnea with activities of daily living, a symptom limited endurance treadmill test, and the Medical Outcomes Study-Short Form (SF-36) to assess self-reported functioning. Over one-third (36) of study participants scored high risk for depression. Overall, all groups showed significant improvement in CES-D scores from baseline to follow up two months later; however, no differences were seen between the groups.

There are some researchers who believe that anxiety affects symptoms of chronic breathing disorders (like COPD) more so than depression. Cully et al. (2006) developed a hypothesis regarding this same belief by stating that anxiety would be responsible for a greater difference than symptoms of depression on symptoms of chronic breathing disorders because breathing distress, by nature, is fear-provoking. This controlled and randomized trial involved 179 individuals diagnosed with COPD and comorbid anxiety and/or depression and was intended to evaluate the use of CB therapy to treat these individuals. Participants completed the BDI to assess depression, the BAI to assess anxiety, the Forced Expiratory Value to assess symptom severity of COPD, a self-report questionnaire regarding medical comorbidity, the CRQ to assess disease specific quality of life, the SF-36 to assess quality of life, and a six-minute walking test to assess physical functioning. Analysis of the data gathered showed that mental health stress (meaning symptoms of anxiety

101

and depressed) explained a significant amount of difference in quality of life. Depression was found to be responsible for a moderate difference on multiple outcome models.

Symptoms of depression may be one of several predictors of how well individuals with COPD will be able to function. Wall (2007) hypothesized that resource variables (coping, well-being, and physiologic) would significantly predict functional performance in community-residing adults. Physiologic variables refer to the severity of COPD, and chronic medical comorbidities. Well-being variables refer to symptoms of depression, anxiety, life satisfaction, and happiness while coping variables refer to environmental coping, perceived social support, and internal coping. The researcher recruited 119 participants and had them complete a Functional Performance Inventory-Short Form (FPI-SF) and the anxiety and depression subscales of the Hospital Anxiety and Depression Scale (HADS-A and HADS-D). Though the hypothesis was not fully supported, four variables (depression, severity of COPD, gender, and age) accounted for 46% of the difference in functional performance.

Literature Limitations

Depression and chronic illness. Eight studies regarding depression and chronic illness (including one or more of the following conditions: respiratory disease, arthritis, heart disease, stroke, diabetes, and hypertension) demonstrated some limitations. Of these studies, four contained small sample sizes, ranging from 90 to 415 subjects. The other two studies included moderate to large sample sizes of 1,801 and 430,912 respondents. In the smaller-sized studies, researchers recruited participants from the following areas: low-income high rise health centers (3) in one southeast U.S. city's retirement communities, (29) in the northeast section of one U.S. state's primary care clinics (19) affiliated with nine health care organizations in five U.S. states, and clinics (12) in a university affiliated primary care network in the Northern region of one U.S. state. Veteran's Health Administration (VHA) claims, Medicare claims, and the 2007 Behavioral Risk Factor Surveillance System account for the number of participants in the large sized studies.

Only three of the chronic illness studies included all adults ages 18 and older. One limited age to 40 and older, and the other four studies limited age to 51 and older. Women made up the majority of participants in all but three of the studies; two studies consisted of all women and the third had nearly equal representation of men and women. In five of the studies, the majority of subjects described themselves as Caucasian; in one study, the majority described themselves as African American, another study most participants identified their country of origin as Central America and in the remaining studies, data on race is not available. Demographics in all but two of the studies were limited to age, gender, and race. Three studies included education (47% having less than a high school education) and marital status (58% non-married which includes never married, divorced/separated, and widowed).

Hu and Gruber (2008) used only one parameter to gauge health status, but other health parameters could have been collected. The PANAS may not adequately represent the full range of potential emotional temperaments. Zausniewski and Bekhet (2009) administered the full version (20-item) of the CES-D to measure depression, and their study does not discuss whether or not there are standardized cutoff scores for the CES-D so that the results of their study can be compared with the shortened version (12-item). Hirsch et al. (2009) gathered data by self-report, creating the potential for biased information regarding participants' medical problems. They used a single item to assess positive emotion and did not provide a more detailed assessment of suicidal ideation. Jerant et al. (2010) developed several hypotheses, increasing the potential for chance findings because of multiple hypotheses testing accounting for the main limitation of their study.

Karakus and Patton (2011) did not discuss any research questions or hypotheses in their study and used a sample of convenience. These researchers used exclusionary criteria for recruitment (only patients who did not report one of four illnesses at study entry) and self-report measures were used (which the researchers' state is a valid and cost efficient method to identify chronic illness). The authors cite the following two study specific limitations: collecting data on subjects involved in all seven waves of the study resulted in the loss of a large number of participants, and they agreed that the selection of only healthy individuals at baseline may have led to an underestimation of the correlation between depression and chronic illness. Maradiegue and Kahn (2013) cited three study specific limitation including a small sample size, lack of a control group, and lack of geographic diversity (only medical records from one CHC in one location selected for review).

Depression and heart disease. Six studies related to depression and heart disease (including angina, heart failure, congestive heart failure, heart attack, and heart transplant) disclose some limitations as well. Half of these studies have small sample sizes ranging from 69 to 104 participants and the other half assess larger sample sizes ranging from 370 to 1306 participants. The number of participants among all samples totaled 2,650. Subjects were recruited from three VA hospitals/clinics (including one in Boston), eight university/community clinical centers (Duke University, Yale University, Washington State University, Stanford University, University of Washington, University of Missouri, University of Alabama-Birmingham, and the Rush-Presbyterian-St. Luke's medical Center), and the Barnes Jewish Hospital nuclear cardiology exercise stress testing lab.

Three studies limited the age of their participants: two required participants to be at least 60 years while one required participants to be at least 21 years of age. The

107

other studies reported age as ranges: 40-90, 47-73, and 53-73 years. Men account for 85% (2,250) of the participants in these six studies while only 400 women (15%) participated. In all but the largest sampled study (which did not assess race/ethnicity), the majority of participants identified race/ethnicity as White or Caucasian (73% or 980 participants) and 27% (or 364 subjects) identified with a minority race/ethnicity.

Four of six studies assessed education level, and three of these measured it as greater than high school and less than high school (69% or 625 had a greater than high school education), and the other study assessed education as an average (the mean education level was 14.1 years with a standard deviation of 2.9 years). As a result, the findings of these studies are difficult to generalize to the larger population of all adults in the United States who experience both depression and heart disease. Two-thirds of the studies (4) measured marital status and income level. Out of 1,275 participants, 58.5% (746) of participants identified themselves as either married or living with partner. In two studies, 102 of 200 participants (51%) had an annual household income greater than $20,000; a third study reported that 37% (224 of 705 participants) had an annual household income greater than $30,000 and the fourth study described income level as being employed (30% or 111 of 370 participants).

Collectively, limitations exist in these studies addressing depression and heart disease, as they do not similarly collect or measure demographic data, which, in turn, diminishes the ability to correlate the prevalence of depression with demographic information such as age, gender, race/ethnicity, education, income and marital status. In the study conducted by Paukert et al. (2009), research questions and hypotheses were not clearly identified. By employing too many (8) measures in a two-hour interview, the researchers created both a risk for fatigue among study participants and the potential for overlapping results. Study-cited limitations include the following: recruiting subjects so that half did not have a diagnosis of either anxiety or depression and half met criteria for anxiety and/or depression as well as collecting data through self-report (a reflection of participant perception instead of objective observation).

Cully et al. (2010), like the researchers above, did not identify their research questions or hypotheses clearly. They cite specific to their study limitations of patient self-selection for participation and brief self-report inventories which they state may have limited their understanding of their relationship to quality of life. Several limitations were noted in the Day et al. (2005) study. The first section contained a poor literature review. The researchers did not discuss the reliability and validity of two of the measures they employed and the third measure (heart disease attributions) was not standardized, provided participants a limited number of possible answers, and was not proven to have reliability or validity. Limitations cited by the researchers include a failure to review medical records, a

110

lack of comparison groups, and the recruiting of subjects while they underwent an exercise stress test.

Lett et al. (2009) cited four specific limitations of their study. The study lacked a control group consisting of non-depressed and non-isolated participants. Only chronic heart disease patients with low social support and/or depression were selected from a convenience sample due to budgetary limits. Over time, as they administered their chosen measures, the number of participants decreased, leading to potentially unreliable estimates. Participants provided data via self-report rather than researchers' collecting data objectively through observation.

While similar limitations are found in the Kubzansky et al. (2006) study, the researchers' sole cited limitation is that results can only be generalized to white men. Rybarczyk et al. (2007) acknowledge that, like the Kubzansky study, one of the limitations of their study is limited minority representation. However, in addition, they state that they faced a higher risk of chance results and

Type I errors because they employed the exploratory statistical method. Two other limitations cited by the Rybarczyk study include non-longitudinal methodology and the medical model perspective of the assessment of adjustment by way of negative affect.

Depression and cancer. Eight studies concerned with depression and cancer (including non-small cell lung cancer, breast cancer, prostate cancer, advanced (or late stage) cancer, and metastatic stage IV cancer) have demonstrated limitations similar to the studies discussed previously. All but one study recruited small sample sizes, ranging from 55 to 289 participants; the last study had a very large sample size of 8,054 participants. The researchers gathered their subjects from hospital/university clinics (at least 8 in Wisconsin, New York, San Francisco, Connecticut, and Washington state), VA hospital clinics (4 in Wisconsin, San Francisco, Connecticut, and a SW U.S. metropolitan area), and radiation clinics (9 in Missouri). Additional participants were selected from a palliative medicine program, a home care service of a community hospital, the Coping with Cancer Study, and the Wisconsin Longitudinal Study.

Participants' (in all but one study) ages were averaged with a standard deviation: collectively, the youngest participants were age 31 and the eldest were age 94 at study entry. Women made up the majority of study participants (4,889 or 55%) while men numbered 4,023 or 45% in six of the studies: two studies did not measure gender. Race/ethnicity was measured in all but one study; the largest study only states that the majority of participants were white. Of the other six studies, 80% (732 of 916 participants) identified themselves as White or Caucasian and 20% (184) identified themselves as belonging to a minority group (including Black/African American, Hispanic/Latino, American Indian/Alaskan Native, Native American, or Asian).

Researchers from six of the eight studies measured education level while half of the studies measured income level and five of the eight studies measured marital status. Fifty-four percent (310) of participants in four studies completed greater than a high school education, and a fifth study compared the average educational level of two subgroups (New York: 16.2 years to San Francisco: 14.1 years), and a sixth study reported the average educational level of its participants as 12.4 years with a standard deviation of 4.1 years. Regarding income, one study stated that 100 (45%) of their 223 participants were employed, a second study revealed that 121 (70.2%) of their 172 participants had an annual income of $30,000 or greater, and two additional studies reported income at median levels of $25,000 (27 or 46.6% of participants made more) and $20,000 to 30,000. The majority of participants (547 or 63.8%) in five studies identified themselves as married or living with a partner.

Among these studies, several limitations overlap (both observed and study-cited). These overlapping limitations include lack of discussion regarding study-specific research questions and/or hypotheses, lack of a control group, use of multiple measures, use of non-standardized measures, and lack of discussion regarding reliability and validity of measures. Additional, limitations shared by two or more these studies consist of self-reported data, small to modest sample sizes, samples of convenience, cross-sectional study design, and lack of representation of minority races. Though not always evaluated for correlations with demographics, sample sizes for the majority of these studies did not represent gender, race/ethnicity, age, education, income, or marital status.

Just as these studies show specific results according to their research design, they also demonstrate study-specific limitations. All studies, with the exception of two, used exclusion criteria for recruitment: only stage IV cancer patients (Else-Quest et al., 2009), only cancer patients with a 6 to 12 month prognosis (Rabkin et al., 2009), only advanced-stage cancer patients (Lichtenthal et al., 2009), only breast cancer patients (Schlegel et al.,

2009), only men (Hoyt et al., 2009), and only patients with early-stage non-small cell lung cancer who underwent surgical resection and who had been actively smoking for three months prior to and at study entry (Walker et al., 2006). The Else-Quest study used abbreviated measures to assess multiple factors in order to decrease the burden of time and energy, increasing the risk of confounding factors' skewing study results. In contrast, the Kirkova et al. (2010) study only used one measure and did not consider the possibility of other factors that may influence study results. In addition, the Kirkova study cited the following limitations as study-specific: short assessment time frames, grouping primary cancer locations, dichotomous measuring of distress, ordering of questions, and participants' engagement in therapy (either prior to or at study entry) which could have influenced study results

Lictenthal et al. (2009) noted a potential for selection bias because they found that the individuals who refused to participate expressed more distress than those who agreed to participate. They also discussed that one of the measures they used, the SCID-I, contains insensitive questions, leading to the possible underestimation of the true prevalence of mental health disorders. Schlegel et al. (2009) stated that their testing of a large number of possible interactions limited the results of their study and their predicted interactions accounted for the small amount of differences. In the Pudrovska (2010) study, the researcher mentioned only one limitation in that the physiological effects of cancer potentially confound study results.

Depression, diabetes and chronic kidney disease. Four studies reviewing the association between depression and diabetes as well as two studies looking at the correlation between depression and chronic kidney disease were conducted between 2006 and 2010. Sample sizes for these six studies ranged from 59 to 998 participants. In two studies 418 individuals diagnosed with chronic kidney disease participated, and, in four studies,

117

1,352 diagnosed with diabetes mellitus participated. Researchers selected participants from two hospital/university clinics (renal medicine in Iowa and diabetes center in Florida), the Native Hawaiian Health Research Project in North Kohala, the CORE Health & Retirement Study (4th and 5th Waves), and a diabetic outpatient clinic. With the exception of one study in which participants had to be eighteen years of age or older, all other study participants' ages were averaged with a standard deviation; the youngest participants were 26 years of age and the eldest participants were 75 years of age.

Collectively among all studies, men and women were nearly equally represented: 916 (51%) men and 865 (49%) women participated. The majority of participants in five studies measuring race/ethnicity identified themselves as White/Caucasian (1,267 or 71%) while the other 29% identified their race/ethnicity as African American, Hispanic, Asian, Native Hawaiian, Filipino, Japanese, Mixed races, or

Other.   Two-thirds of these studies did not consider measuring educational level as a potential confounding factor: two studies did measure it as an average (12.4 years with a standard deviation of 2.6 years and 12.81 years with a standard deviation of 2.69 years).   None of these studies measured income level and only one study measured marital status (38 or 64% of participants identified as being married or living with a partner).

Several of these studies share two or more of the following limitations: small sample size, no discussion of study-specific research questions or hypotheses, cross-sectional design, use of self-report measures, and little representation of minority races.   Each study, with the exception of two, used exclusion criteria in their selection of participants such as only individuals with chronic kidney disease with a creatinine level over 3.0 mg/dL, not on dialysis and never had a kidney transplant (Hoth et al., 2006).   Kellerman et al. (2010) selected participants only if they had a creatinine level of 2.5 mg/dL or later.   Chiu et al.

119

(2010) and Kaholokula et al. (2006) both required participants to be diagnosed with Type 2 diabetes.

Hoth et al. (2006) recognized two additional limitations specific to their study, stating that they did not control for other possible clinical factors, and they used change in depression as the only measure of adjustment. In their study, Kellerman et al. (2010) acknowledged selection bias as a limitation. The inability to determine a causal direction, a five-year time lapse between assessments, the potential for other behavioral factors to affect results, and only being able to generalize results to middle-aged and older adults with depressive symptoms are all limitations reported by Chiu et al. (2010). Sacco and Yanover (2006) cited three limitations specific to their study: they did not evaluate factors inherently involved in their hypotheses, medical symptoms may have been reported under a bias of depression (negatively), and their results cannot be generalized to other populations of adults with diabetes. A significant limitation of the Daly et al.

120

(2007) study is that they did not discuss any limitations specific to their study. Kaholokula et al. (2006) stated that they limited their study by only looking at some features of the Health Related Quality of Life measure and also by only using one measure for each construct as they believe that using multiple measures reduces the likelihood of errors in measurement.

Depression and arthritis. Two studies looked at the connection between depression and rheumatoid arthritis with sample sizes ranging from 138-344 individuals. A total of 482 individuals recruited by physician referral and the UCSF RA Panel Study of 1995 participated in these two studies. One study measured age by gender (mean age for women was 51.7 years and mean age for men was 60 years), and the other study measured age for both genders (the youngest participants were 48 years, and the eldest were 75 years old). The majority of participants were women (340 or 70.5%) and White/Caucasian (392 or 81%). One study measured educational level (average of

121

13.2 years with a standard deviation of 2.9 years), one study measured marital status (264 of 344 participants or 77% identified themselves as being married or living with a partner), and neither study measured income level as a potential confounding factor.

Both of these studies share several limitations: consisting of mostly female participants, poor representation of minority races, excluding criteria for participation to individuals with rheumatoid arthritis, and utilizing multiple self-report measures. Further limitations observed of the Zautra et al. (2007) study include not using a control group and not discussing the reliability and validity of stress-induction interventions. The researchers cite specifically that they limited their study through the selection of a small sample, the use of a retrospective design, and not considering how the results may have been influenced by sleep quantity/quality and anxiety. Morris et al. (2008) note that their study contains "several limitations" but only discuss one: they did not obtain a clinical assessment of their participants at study entry.

Depression and chronic lung disease. Engaging the participation of 636 individuals, four studies explored the relationship between depression and Chronic Obstructive Pulmonary Disease (COPD). Each study contained a small sample size, ranging from 100 to 238 participants recruited from the Michael E. DeBakey VA Medical Center in Texas, a private pulmonary medicine practice, physician referrals, and the Better Breathing Club of the American Lung Association. Of the four studies, one limited age to 40 years and older while the other three measured age as an average with a standard deviation: the youngest participants were 55 years of age and the eldest participants were 78 years old. The majority of subjects were men (515 or 81%); women made up 19% (or 121) of the total sample size. Three of the four studies measured race/ethnicity and the majority (85% or 454) of 536 participants identified themselves and White/Caucasian, leaving minorities (including

Black/African American and Hispanic) accounting for 15% of the sample sizes. None of these four studies measured education level, income level, or marital status as potential confounding factors.

All of these studies relating to depression and lung disease have at least two of the following limitations in common: exclusionary recruitment criteria of only patients diagnosed with COPD, no discussion of specific to study research questions or hypotheses, no control group for comparison, use of self-report measures, small convenience sample sizes, and poor representation of minority races. Kunik et al. (2008) as well as Cully et al. (2006) used another exclusionary criterion requiring individuals to have a diagnosis of depression and/or anxiety. Low recruitment, their delivery of interventions, the selection of only military veterans as participants, and their lack of documentation regarding changes in psychotropic and COPD medications throughout the study are specific limitations cited by these researchers.

124

Cully et al. (2006) state they limited their study with a methodological design which kept them from being able to prove causality and with their selection bias (primarily male military veterans). While the Wall (2007) study did not cite the limitation of using a cross-sectional design, it did cite several other study-specific limitations. These limitations include lack of geographic diversity, individuals with undiagnosed COPD or without access to healthcare not included in the study, no assessment completed of positive and negative affect, exclusion of symptoms (including dyspnea and fatigue) as confounding factors, lack of pulmonary functioning tests, and a time lapse (418 days) between data collection times. Nguyen and Carrieri-Kohlman (2005) did not discuss the reliability and validity of their chosen interventions and they did not cite any study specific limitations.

Research Method and Procedures

A systematic review of the literature on the relationship between depression and chronic medical illness was conducted to 1) explore the prevalence of depression and co-morbid chronic medical illness, 2) identify the instruments used to assess depressive symptoms, and 3) discover potentially effective treatment modalities for individuals with co-depression and chronic medical illness. The author examined multiple studies to discern their appropriateness for inclusion in this review and then evaluate the methodological quality of those selected studies. Searches were completed on the following behavioral sciences electronic databases: ProQuest Psychology Journals, PsycARTICLES, Psychology and Behavioral Sciences Collection, and PsycEXTRA.

Relevant articles were searched for by using the following keywords: depression and chronic illness, depression and heart disease, depression and diabetes, depression and chronic kidney disease, depression and cancer, depression and arthritis, depression and lung disease, Beck Depression Inventory validity, Center for

Epidemiological Studies – Depression validity, Geriatric Depression Scale validity, and the Patient Health Questionnaire validity. This search was limited primarily to studies published between 2006 and 2011 with the exception of a few studies older than 2006. I also limited the studies to include only those conducted within the United States with at least 50 participants who were eighteen years of age or older. Selected studies must have included the prevalence of depression among individuals with at least one of the top eight chronic medical illnesses: heart disease, diabetes, cancer, arthritis, cholesterol, kidney disease and lung disease.

Methodology

The method to study depression and chronic illness was to summarize and interpret findings in recent literature. In doing so, this author reviewed numbers of participants diagnosed with depression, the most popular valid and reliable depression screening tools, researchers' discussion of risk factors for developing depression, and researchers' attempts to evaluate various psychological treatment interventions. This author examined studies conducted by numerous researchers to answer the research questions regarding the relationship between depression and chronic illness, risk factors, and the most effective screening tools and psychological interventions. In addition, this author drew conclusions about the importance of this research to the field of psychology as well as recommended directions for future research.

Data Analysis

In analyzing the data, this author placed a greater importance in studies that report the number of participants diagnosed with depression who have at least one chronic illness. Well-controlled studies with control groups offered more accurate conclusions about the relationship between depression and chronic illness. Studies able to replicate results proved to have greater significance than isolated studies. However, in the quest to gather well-controlled research studies, this author discovered there were a limited number in existence on the topic of depression and chronic illness. Among these studies, very few of them actually replicate results of previous studies, but, rather, are isolated studies. As a result, this author was limited to the conclusions that can be drawn from the findings of this research study.

Assumptions

The theoretical framework of this study is assumed to be sound; early screening, accurate diagnosis, and effective treatment of depression can decrease morbidity and improve quality of life as well as the management of chronic illness. This author assumed that the variables have been clearly defined and are measurable: studies administer standardized screening tools and report the number of participants who scored high enough to be diagnosed with depression, allowing this author to determine the prevalence of depression among all participants in these studies. Depression screening tools have been proven to be valid and reliable, as discussed in the literature review, allowing this author to assume this study's variables are measurable. Regarding participants, this author assumed that these studies recruited participants who represent the population, willingly participated, and answered questions without bias as much as possible. This author assumed that the results of this study can be generalized to the general population, suggesting that there is a significant correlation between depression and chronic illness beyond the samples in these studies. Results of this study will be meaningful to the field of psychology and other mental health professionals, as they realize the importance of early detection and effective treatment in patients with depression and chronic illness.

Methodological Assumptions and Limitations

In analyzing these many research studies, this author first assumed that the inconsistent use of depression screening tools across all 34 studies is insufficient to determine an accurate prevalence of depression in patients with chronic illness. Each depression screening tool has its strengths and weaknesses, and each may not measure depression or depressive symptoms in the same way as the others. True scientific research involves the repeated replication of results; this means that, to be true science, these studies would have used the exact same screening tools to measure depression or depressive symptoms. This author understood that not all studies are the same, and, because of this, some studies will be more scientifically-based.

Secondly, this researcher assumed that all studies took into consideration potential confounding factors that may account for the differences in depression among patients with chronic physical illness. In the effort to find a true relationship between depression and chronic illness, researchers must seek to control these confounding factors as much as possible. This author understood that, due to time constraints, financial constraints, and limited resources, the control of confounding factors was not

131

always possible. Therefore, it is difficult generalize findings to a larger population when study results may have been influenced by other factors.

Several methodological limitations could be found in these studies' small sample sizes. Some studies set limits on age while the others considered adults age 18 and over. Women made up the majority of participants in fifteen studies, men in ten studies, and two studies did not report gender information. The majority of participants identified themselves as Caucasian/White; minorities were not well-represented. Regarding education, marital status, and income level (all of which have been named as risk factors for developing depression), the majority of these studies did not consider these demographics as potential confounding factors. Though the majority of these studies gathered demographics on two or more of the six demographic types (age, gender, race/ethnicity, education, marital status and income), nearly all of them failed to look at potential correlations with symptoms of depression and chronic illness

Limitations of the Study

This study was limited by the small number of studies that address this researcher's questions related to depression and such chronic medical illnesses as heart disease, cancer, arthritis, lung disease, diabetes and kidney disease. Viewing them collectively as chronic medical illnesses, many studies have been gathered for use in this study. However, generalizing results to the larger population of all adults with at least one chronic medical illness is difficult because, though similar in some regards, they do not all agree in the instruments used to measure depression, the statistical methods used to analyze data or the interpretations of their findings. One important aspect that they do agree on is the importance of understanding how depression and chronic medical illness affect one another so that appropriate and effective treatment methods can be explored and implemented.

Chapter Three: Research Findings

Summary

Recognizing the impact depression has on physical health and the power of psychological interventions to counter that impact is a critical need for every individual living in America. Health care and health care reform is a hot topic and, for many Americans, affordable health care seems elusive. The talking points of the health care reform debate focus on coverage for everyone, deciding who should be treated and when, health care as a right, and waste and fraud. Unfortunately, the impact of mental health on physical health, effective psychological interventions, and the potential of those interventions to reduce the cost of health care has not entered into the debate.

Seven years prior to this study, the Centers for Disease Control and Prevention (2010) reported that 133 million Americans suffered with at least one chronic illness. Approximately 61.1 million battled some type of mental health disorder every year (NAMI, 2011). Shockingly, over half of depressed patients in primary care settings were going without detection and treatment (Maradiegue & Khan, 2013). In the not so distant future (2020), it is predicted that depression will be second only to heart disease (Chapman et al., 2005) and the leading cause of disability among women (NAMI, 2011). Empowering individuals to manage depression will also provide them the ability to manage chronic illness.

Quality of life is significantly affected because of the functional limitations imposed on individuals by the symptoms of depression and chronic illness. Arthritis, heart disease, cancer, kidney disease, diabetes and lung disease are among the most diagnosed chronic illnesses. Add depression to any combination of these illnesses, and primary care and emergency visits increase, inpatient hospitalizations increase, and efforts to self-manage illness decrease. Depression screening, psychotropic medication and psychotherapy have the potential to increase self-management of illness and decrease the utilization of various health care services.

The purpose of this study was fourfold: to examine the relationship between depression and chronic physical illness, to review screening tools for depression, to discover risk factors of developing depression, and to investigate potential biopsychosocial interventions. To reach these goals, this study sought to answer the following questions.

1) What relationship exists between chronic physical illness and symptoms of depression?
2) What methods are used to screen for depressive symptoms and when is the best time to conduct screenings?
3) What risk factors exist that predict the development of depression or depressive symptoms?
4) What psychological interventions impact symptoms of depression among individuals who have been diagnosed with or self-report at least one chronic illness?

Results of this study have the potential to influence how and which services are provided by medical and mental health professionals alike. It may also provide justification for insurance companies to cover the cost of psychological interventions that will effectively decrease the utilization of emergency rooms and hospitalizations. The first intention of this study was to review scholarly journal articles related to the relationship between depression and chronic physical illness. Secondly, this study intended to analyze similarities and differences between the results of this study and the results discovered by the studies included in the scholarly journal articles.

The following behavioral sciences electronic databases were used to gather articles pertinent to the purposes of this study: ProQuest Psychology Journals, PsycArticles, Psychology and Behavioral Sciences Collection, and PsycEXTRA. Using keywords such as depression and chronic illness, depression and heart disease, depression and diabetes, depression and chronic kidney disease, depression and cancer, depression and arthritis, depression and lung disease, Beck Depression Inventory validity, Center for Epidemiological Studies – Depression validity, Geriatric Depression Scale validity and the Patient Health Questionnaire validity, studies published

137

primarily between 2006 and 2013 were selected for review. In addition, selected studies were limited to those conducted only in the United States with at least 50 participants aged eighteen and older. They needed to have included the prevalence of depression among individuals with at least one of eight chronic illnesses.

For the purposes of this study, chronic illness was defined as the presence of a recognized medical illness as the result of a disease process that has no cure and requires ongoing life-long health care treatment. Depression is characterized as a mental illness as defined by specific symptoms in the DSM-IV-TR. Depressive symptoms are the symptoms of a Major Depressive Disorder as explained by the DSM-IV-TR, but not severe enough to meet criteria for a diagnosis of Major Depressive Disorder. An adult is any individual over eighteen years of age.

Literature review. Primary care providers fail to recognize and treat anywhere from 35 to 70% of adults with depressive disorders (Thomas & Brantley, 2004). This lack of detection generated a need for more efficient, routine screening tools. Most primary care providers cite the amount of time needed for and the difficulty of administration as the top barriers to use in their practices. In addition, patient negative reaction and physician's sensitivity to stigmatization of patients influence their hesitance to use current screening methods (Scogin & Shah, 2006).

There is no doubt that identifying depression will help individuals manage and improve their health and functioning (Friedman et al., 2005). Screening methods center on the use of self-report questionnaires (Brown & Shinka, 2005). Several criticisms of self-report measures have been expressed by researchers across the globe. Some tools ask about somatic symptoms which may not only be related to depression but can also be the result of a physical disorder (Wancata et al., 2006). Questions may be suitable for younger people but could cause difficulties

139

for the elderly. Individuals with impaired cognitive functioning may be confused by the response format and unable to answer many if not most of the questions.

Despite their criticisms, self-report questionnaires have gained popularity. Providers like them because they can be administered and scored in a relatively short amount of time (Merz et al., 2011). Though diagnostic interviews have been shown to be the most effective and accurate way of identifying depression and depressive symptoms, clinicians in primary care settings do not have the proper amount of time to engage in this type of assessment. The four more popular screening tools include the BDI-II, the CES-D, the GDS, and the PHQ-9.

The BDI-II was developed to be more closely in tune with the diagnostic criteria of Major Depressive Disorder as discussed in the DSM-IV-TR (Quilty et al., 2010). It is a 21-item questionnaire in which respondents rate frequency of symptoms on a four-point Likert scale and with a potential score of 63 (Dutton et al., 2005); higher scores reflect more severe depression (Quilty et al., 2010). Research does demonstrate that the BDI-II has good psychometric properties, high internal consistency, good test-retest reliability, and good construct and concurrent validity (Dutton et al., 2005). Its usefulness has been proven valid for outpatient psychiatric care, primary care patients, inpatient geriatric patients, college students, and psychiatric outpatient adolescents; however, the majority of respondents have been middle class Caucasian individuals.

The CES-D, primary used in the research field, is a 20-item questionnaire that examines symptoms from the previous week (Edwards et al., 2010). Critics state the CES-D is too long to be used as a screening tool in medical and rehabilitation settings (Martens et al., 2006). Scores on this measure consider four components: depressed affect, positive affect, somatic and retarded activity, and interpersonal relationships. It has been proven valid among urban residents; married men and women; primary

141

care patients; university students; English- and Spanish-speaking individuals in psychiatric outpatient care; White, Black, Hispanic, and Mexican American adults; community-living adults; adult women; patients with rheumatoid arthritis; ethnically diverse individuals; and older adults.

A popular screening tool with the elderly (Lopez et al., 2010), the GDS, is a validated 30-item scale designed to assist with the differentiation of depression from dementia (Brown & Shinka, 2005). Some criticize its assessment of somatic symptoms because of the potential to confound a diagnosis of depression with a physical illness common among the elderly (Friedman et al., 2005). The shortened form (15-item) was developed for medical professionals concerned with time-constraints and for use with people who express significant fatigue (Brown & Shinka, 2005). Many researchers believe the GDS is an unreliable measure with individuals with dementia, as poor memory can lead to guessing (Lopez et al., 2010). Older adults find this screening tool to be acceptable, not too

142

stressful and not difficult to complete (Scogin & Shah, 2006).

The most popular tool used in primary care settings is the PHQ-9, a 9-item questionnaire that takes about five minutes to complete and one minute to score (Merz et al., 2011). These items do correlate with the symptoms of Criterion A for Major Depressive Episode as described in the DSM-IV-TR (Cannon et al., 2007). Respondents rate the frequency (over a two week period) of the following nine symptoms on a four-point Likert scale: anhedonia, depressed mood, sleep difficulties, fatigue, changes in appetite, feelings of worthlessness or guilt, difficulty concentrating, motor agitation, and suicidal ideation (Merz et al., 2011). Higher scores equal greater severity of depressive symptoms.

Thirty-four scholarly journal articles related to the prevalence of depression and chronic illness met inclusion criteria for this author's study. Five of these articles expressed their only concern was to determine the prevalence of depression among their chosen subjects. In a descriptive study, the reliability and validity of the CES-D was examined by evaluating whether elderly women with chronic conditions can be diagnosed with depression based on the cut-off scores of 12 shortened measures (Zauszniewski & Bekhet, 2009). Shen et al. (2010) wanted to compare the rates of major and minor depression in female veterans diagnosed with at least one of three specified chronic illnesses. Older veterans with heart failure were also selected in a study to review factors associated with depression in order to improve detection and appropriate treatments (Paukert et al., 2009). With patients diagnosed with advanced-stage cancer, Lictenthal et al. (2009) investigated the rate of development of mental disorders as they neared death. Besides evaluating the prevalence of depression in a diabetic outpatient population, Daly et al. (2007) looked at the screening process and questioned whether there was a significant difference between those with depression and those without on the control of blood sugar levels.

Using a cut-off score of 16 on the CES-D, 38.5% of participants in the Zauszniewski & Bekhet (2009) study met criteria to be diagnosed with depression. Shen et al. (2010) found that women with diabetes or diabetes and hypertension had higher rates of MDD than those with hypertension only; adults 75 years of age and older were found to be more likely to have unspecified depression or minor depression than those adults younger than 50 years of age who were more likely to have MDD. While looking at the factors associated with depression, Paukert et al. (2009) discovered that participants in the depressed group were significantly more depressed, more anxious, more physically limited by heart failure, more intrusive, more maladaptive in coping responses, more likely to attribute control to chance and more likely to have lower self-efficacy than the non-depressed group. Apparently, impending death was not a significant factor, as the findings of Lichtenthal et al. (2009) indicate the prevalence of mental illness did not increase or decrease as participants neared death. Daly et al. (2007) reported that 37.1% of their participants demonstrated evidence of MDD and 27% exhibited depressive symptoms not severe enough for any depression diagnosis.

The common theme of quality of life as it relates to depression was shared by 17 of the 34 selected scholarly articles. Older adults with positive affect, subjective happiness, or certain personality traits may demonstrate fewer chronic illness symptoms, less pain, less distress, and better quality of life while those with negative affect may express greater pain, increased symptoms, decreased functioning, increased distress, self-blame, increased stigma, poorer adjustment and poorer quality of life (Chen et al., 2011; Cully et al., 2010; Day et al., 2005; Else-Quest et al., 2009; Hirsch et al., 2009; Hu & Gruber, 2008; Jerant et al., 2010; Kaholokula et al., 2006; Kirkova et al., 2010; Kubzansky et al., 2006; Kunik et al., 2008; Pudrovska, 2010; Rabkin et al., 2009; Rybarczyk et al., 2007; Schlegel et al., 2009; Wall, 2007; Zautra et al., 2007). Five articles look specifically at the prevalence of depression among elderly women with chronic conditions, female veterans with at least one chronic condition, older veterans with heart failure, patients with advanced-stage cancer approaching death, and diabetic outpatient populations (Daly et al., 2007; Lichtenthal et al., 2009; Paukert et al., 2009; Shen et al., 2010; Zauszniewski & Bekhet, 2009).

The relationship between social support and depression was evaluated in four articles regarding their impact on mortality and morbidity, coping styles, symptoms of diabetes, and agreeableness as these pertains to chronic kidney disease (Hoth et al., 2007; Lett et al., 2009; Sacco & Yanover, 2006; Walker et al., 2006). In the eight remaining articles, the authors look at the impact depression has on the development of chronic illness, the control of chronic conditions including blood sugar levels, functioning, utilization of health services, sleep quality, mortality, dyspnea, and COPD (Chiu et al., 2010; Cully et al., 2006; Hoyt et al., 2009; Karakus & Patton, 2011; Kellerman et al., 2010; Maradiegue & Khan, 2013; Morris et al., 2008; Nguyen & Carrieri-Kohlman, 2005). For the purposes of this study, all of these 34 articles provided this author with numbers of individuals diagnosed with depression, potential risk factors for developing depression, the tools used to assess depression, and a few discussed possible treatment interventions. Those findings are discussed in depth later in this chapter.

A summary of the findings of the studies mentioned above is presented in the following paragraphs as they pertain to this project. The Five Factor Model personality traits did not prove to have a significant relationship with levels of distress (Jerant et al., 2010) but Kubzansky et al. (2006) did find distress to be associated with greater risk of coronary heart disease. Caucasians showed higher distress levels and depressed symptoms than did African Americans (Hu & Gruber, 2008). Hirsch et al. (2009) found a significant positive association between suicidal ideation and mood disorder severity; distress associated with suicidal ideation increased as the number of chronic illnesses increased however that distress appeared to be moderated by happiness.

Sadness and stress have been named among the top eleven attributed causes of heart disease (Day et al., 2005). According to Chen et al. (2011), participants with up to one chronic illness expressed a higher prevalence of mental distress than physical distress, those with two or more chronic conditions demonstrated greater physical distress than mental distress, and those with three or more conditions were more likely to report poor quality of life than those with one or two conditions. Depression is correlated with a reduction in quality of life, greater impairment in physical abilities, heart failure symptom frequency, symptom burden, and social functioning (Cully et al., 2010); Rybarczyk et al. (2007) discovered that 19% of their participants showed clinically significant depression scores.

Cancer patients demonstrated higher levels of

depression at the beginning of their study than at the two later data collection times, and physical health was positively associated with depressive symptoms at all data collection times (Schlegel et al., 2009). Pudrovska (2010) discovered that participants who did not have a cancer diagnosis at the first data collection but did at the second data collection reported more depressive symptoms than those without cancer, and men with cancer expressed more depressive symptoms than did women. Perceived stigma and self-blame seem to be significant predictors of depression in cancer patients; those who attribute self-blame to the cause of their cancer showed higher rates of depression (Else-Quest et al., 2009). Kirkova et al. (2010) found that participants with the worst performance scores exhibited more clinically important depression while women expressed a higher prevalence of distress over their depression than men.

Stronger spiritual beliefs lessen anxiety, increase hopefulness, facilitate a greater positive mood, and contribute to a better overall satisfaction of life (Rabkin et al., 2009). In addition, participants expressing a positive mood also noted a positive correlation with spiritual beliefs, hope, pleasure, desire to live and overall satisfaction with life as well as a negative correlation with depression, distress and anxiety. Among ethnic groups, Kaholokula et al. (2006) found that those individuals who expressed more symptoms of depression also demonstrated a significant decrease in physical functioning, general health perception, and progression of disease as well as more severe and limiting pain, less energy and more emotional problems that affect work and other activities of daily living. Participants with multiple episodes of depression reported more pain than those who had up to one depressive episode; perceived stress was significantly higher for those with multiple depressive episodes (Zautra et al., 2007).

Cognitive behavioral treatment and COPD education significantly improved BDI and BAI scores, six-minute walking distance, symptoms of anxiety and depression, and quality of life (Kunik et al., 2008). These improvements were maintained for at least 44 weeks. The results of the Wall (2007) study did not fully support its hypothesis that resource variables (coping, well-being, and physiologic) would predict functional performance. These variables did, however, account for 46% of the difference in functional performance.

Social support is believed to make a significant difference for individuals diagnosed with depression and chronic illness in four of the selected scholarly articles for this author's study. Low social support contributes to coronary heart disease by increasing risk for morbidity and mortality (Lett et al., 2009). Walker et al. (2006) reviewed the depressive symptoms of patients newly diagnosed with lung cancer, as they influence coping styles and social support. In a negative cycle, low social support increases depressive symptoms, which increase symptoms of diabetes, and diabetes symptoms increase depressive symptoms, which decrease social support. Also, diabetes

152

symptoms decrease social support, which increases symptoms of depression (Sacco & Yanover, 2006). Hoth et al. (2007) constructed the theory that, for individuals with chronic kidney disease and who score high in agreeableness, greater social support would be associated with less depressive symptoms over time, and, for those with low agreeableness, social support would have little influence on depressive symptoms.

The researchers of these four scholarly articles reported interesting findings. Depression and social support proved to be multidimensional constructs best explained by several underlying factors including cognitive and affective symptoms, somatic symptoms, anxiety symptoms, perceived emotional/intimate support, perceived tangible/peripheral support, children network support, relatives' network support and friends' network support (Lett et al., 2009). Walker et al. (2006) found, at baseline, that depressive symptoms demonstrated a significant association with depressive symptoms at later times while social support correlated significantly with symptoms of depression over time. In addition, depressive symptoms did facilitate the impact of social support on diabetes symptoms and the effects of diabetes symptoms on social support (Sacco & Yanover, 2006). For participants with comorbid chronic kidney disease, individual differences in agreeableness and social support correlated with symptoms of depression; as the researchers expected, for those who scored high on agreeableness, greater social support led to a decrease in depressive symptoms over time, and for, those who scored low, social support proved to have little impact (Hoth et al., 2007).

The final eight scholarly articles selected for this study focus on the impact that depression has on developing chronic illness, comorbid chronic illness, sleep quality, blood-sugar levels, mortality, psychosocial risk, physical functioning, utilization of health services, dyspnea and symptoms of COPD. Karakus and Patton (2011) postulated that depression would influence the number of chronic illnesses and the development of at least one of these four illnesses: arthritis, heart problems/stroke, diabetes, and/or cancer. Sleep quality of cancer patients may be affected by depression (Hoyt et al., 2009). Control of blood-sugar levels in people with Type 2 diabetes may also be associated with depressive symptoms (Chiu et al., 2010).

Symptoms of depression seem to affect the mortality rate of patients with chronic kidney disease (Kellerman et al., 2010). Morris et al. (2008) believed that inadequate psychosocial resources would increase the risk for poor long-term effects including greater depressive symptoms, increased utilization of medical services, greater pain perceptions and increased limitations on physical functioning. Depression would also be associated with dyspnea management but would have less of a role influencing symptoms of COPD than anxiety (Cully et al., 2006; Nguyen & Carrieri-Kohlman, 2005). It is because of the impact depression has on chronic illness that

Maradiegue and Khan (2013) believe controlling depression will provide patients with the ability to control other chronic conditions; this can be done through adequate screening for depression including factors that put them at risk, an effective measurement tool, and family history of illness.

In their study, Karakus and Patton (2011) did find that depression correlated significantly with three of four chronic illnesses and increased the reporting of arthritis, heart problems and diabetes. Symptoms of depression interfered with sleep and the severity of sleep difficulties for men diagnosed with cancer (Hoyt et al., 2009). Though 75% of their sample scored moderately to severely depressed, Chiu et al. (2010) found that health behaviors did not entirely account for the link between depressive symptoms and control of blood-sugar levels while those with low levels of depression did associate with non-compliance to their diabetes treatment plans. More than half of the participants in the Kellerman et al. (2010) study indicated at least mild depressive symptoms and depression scores showed significant correlation with higher mortality risk.

Psychosocial resources placed 133 participants at high risk, 192 at moderate risk, and 236 at low risk for poor long-term outcomes in the Morris et al. (2008) study. As a result, the researchers recommend cognitive behavioral treatment with an emphasis on coping skills and strengthening social support systems. Regarding the management of dyspnea, though the two treatment groups did not differ from each other, they did show significant improvement in their CES-D scores from baseline to follow-up, suggesting that cognitive behavioral treatment and COPD education play an important role in decreasing symptoms of depression (Nguyen & Carrieri-Kohlman, 2005). Cully et al. (2006) reported that mental health stress, in the form of symptoms of anxiety and depression, accounted for a significant difference in quality of life for individuals managing COPD; depression demonstrated responsibility for a moderate difference on outcomes.

Maradiegue and Khan (2013) made three very important discoveries. Health care providers did not document the use of any depressions screening tool. Individuals diagnosed with depression by the physicians did receive treatment (medication and psychotherapy). Unfortunately, many patients at risk are walking out of the primary care setting with unnoticed and untreated depression. Risk factors shared in these scholarly articles include functional impairment, poor health, perceived lack of social support, female, family history of mental illness, impoverishment, financial strain, significant life changes, pregnancy and post pregnancy, social isolation, somatic complaints, substance abuse, older age, loss of sex drive, chronic pain, diagnosis of two or more chronic illnesses, anxiety, anger, mental stress, and other psychosocial problems (Day et al., 2005; Maradiegue & Khan, 2013; Zauszniewski & Bekhet, 2009).

Despite the importance of the findings of these

studies, they do also contain several limitations. Twenty-six studies contain small sample sizes. Nine studies set limits for age requirements while the other studies considered adults age eighteen and over in agreement with the definition of adult for this study. Women made up the majority of participants in fifteen studies, men in ten studies, and two studies did not report gender information.

In twenty-eight studies, the majority of participants identified themselves as Caucasian/White; one study reported a majority of African Americans, one reported a majority with a country of origin as Central America, and four studies did not discuss race/ethnicity. Fifteen studies gathered information on education (in seven of these studies the majority had a high school education or higher and in the other eight they averaged educational level to be greater than high school) and nineteen did not report educational levels. Thirteen studies reported that a majority of their participants were married or living with a partner and twenty-one studies did not gather information on marital status. Only eight studies asked participants about income (four had incomes greater than $30,000 annually, two reported median incomes of $25,000 and $20,000 to $30,000, and two noted that the majority of their participants were unemployed) and the other twenty-six studies did not evaluate income levels. Though the majority of these studies gathered demographics on two or more of the six demographic types (age, gender, race/ethnicity, education, marital status and income), nearly all of them failed to look at potential correlations with symptoms of depression and chronic illness.

Several studies shared two more or more of the following limitations: lack of discussion regarding their research questions/hypotheses, lack of a control group, use of multiple measures, use of non-standardized measures, lack of discussion regarding reliability and validity of their chosen measures, self-report measures, samples of convenience, cross-sectional study design, lack of geographic diversity and use of exclusionary criteria for participant recruitment.   Additionally, many of the researchers described limitations specific to their studies. Hirsch et al. (2009) stated their study was limited by their use of a single-item assessment of positive emotion and they did not provide a detailed assessment of suicidal ideation.   Only one parameter was used to measure health status by Hu and Gruber (2008).   Jerant et al. (2010) reported they limited their study because of multiple hypotheses increasing the potential for chance findings. The collection of data from all seven Waves of assessment resulted in the loss of a large number of participants that could have contributed to the Karakus and Patton (2011) study.

Recruiting participants while they underwent a stress test and failing to review medical records are study-cited limitations by Day et al. (2005).   Cully et al. (2010) expressed that patient self-selection for participation limited the results of their study.   A higher risk of chance results and Type I errors occurred for Rybarczyk et al. (2007)

because they employed the exploratory statistical method. They also cite the use of a non-longitudinal study design and medical model perspective of adjustment via negative affect as limitations.

Else-Quest et al. (2009) cite their use of abbreviated measures to assess multiple factors as a limitation in their study. Short assessment time frames, grouping primary cancer locations, dichotomous measuring of distress, ordering of questions on their measures and participants engagement in therapy are study limitations described by Kirkova et al. (2010). The potential for selection bias in the Lichtenthal et al. (2009) study existed because the individuals who refused to participate expressed more distress than those who agreed to participate. In addition, the researchers discovered that one measure they used contained insensitive questions potentially leading to underestimated results. Schlegel et al. (2009) reported their testing of a large number of possible interactions limited their results and their predicted interactions explained the small amount of differences while Pudrovska (2010) believed it possible that the physiological effects of cancer confounded study results.

Among the studies related to depression and diabetes or chronic kidney disease, Hoth et al. (2006) stated they did not control for other potential clinical factors and they used depression as the only measure of adjustment which potentially affected study findings. Chiu et al. (2010) cited several limitations including the inability to determine a causal direction, a five-year time lapse between assessments, the potential for other behavioral factors to affect study results and only being able to generalize results to middle aged and older adults with symptoms of depression. Conversely, Sacco and Yanover (2006) expressed that they could not generalize study results to other populations of adults with diabetes as they limited their study by failing to evaluate factors inherently involved in their hypotheses and failing to recognize that medical symptoms may have been reported under a bias of

163

depression. Kaholokula et al. (2006) believed that they limited the results of their study by only looking at some of the features of the Health Related Quality of Life measure.

One study stated it contained several limitations but only discussed this one: they did not obtain a clinical assessment of their participants at study entry (Morris et al., 2008). The use of a retrospective design and the lack of consideration regarding how results may have been influenced by sleep quantity, sleep quality and anxiety are two study-specific limitations cited by Zautra et al. (2007). Several limitations reported by Wall (2007) include lack of geographic diversity, no assessment completed of positive and negative affect, exclusion of symptoms as confounding factors, lack of pulmonary functioning tests, time lapse between data collection times, and excluding individuals with undiagnosed COPD or without access to healthcare. Kunik et al. (2008) found low recruitment, their delivery of interventions, and their lack of documentation regarding any changes in psychotropic and/or COPD medications limited their study findings. Finally, an issue that many of these studies possessed but is only documented by one study is that the methodological study design prevented researchers from proving causality between depression and chronic illness and specific to this one study, COPD (Cully et al., 2006).

Results. The study conducted by this author did not intend to look for a causal relationship between depression and chronic illness but, rather, the prevalence of depression in adults with chronic illness, the tools used to measure depression, and potential interventions that could decrease depression. Thirty-four scholarly articles met criteria for inclusion in this study. The total number of participants equaled 465,382. Despite the risks for developing depression discussed previously, these studies did not examine potential differences in these five demographics: gender, race/ethnicity, marital status, education, and income. The compilation of data for this study (Appendix A) relating to these demographic factors

165

bears justification for the future exploration of differences in depressive symptoms.

Two studies (5.9%) did not gather data on gender while 32 studies (94.1%) reported the majority (52.2%) of their participants (n=465,143) identified themselves as female. Twenty-eight studies (82.4%) collected data on race/ethnicity and reported the majority (69.2%) of their participants (n=453,881) as Caucasian/White and the other six studies (17.6%) did not collect data on race/ethnicity. Information gleaned from 19 studies (55.9%) on marital status reveals that the majority (60.3%) of their subjects (n=451,359) identified themselves as married or living with a partner while the remaining 15 studies (44.1%) did not ask about marital status. Educational levels assessed by 16 studies (47%) demonstrated that the majority (88.6%) of their participants (n=438,926) had a high school or greater education, seven studies (20.6%) evaluated educational level as an average ranging from 12.4 years to 15.15 years, and eleven studies (32.4%) did not request information on education.

The least consistently measured demographic across all 34 studies is income status. Twenty studies (58.8%) never collected data on income while 14 studies (41.2%) categorized income either by a numerical annual amount, mean income, median income or employment status. One study reported that 94.8% of participants (n=153) had an annual household income of less than $10,000, two studies reported that 54% of participants (n=3,744) had an annual household income of less than $20,000, two studies indicated that 22% of participants (n=431,050) had an annual household income of less than $25,000, and two studies showed that 60.7% of participants (n=877) had an annual household income of less than $30,000. One study expressed that 41.7% of participants (n=96) noted an annual household income between $10,000 and $20,000. Four studies measured income either by mean ($37,171 and $35,000 to $45,000) or median ($25,000 and $20,000 to $30,000). In the last two studies, 36.5% of participants (n=460) were employed, 60% were unemployed and 3.5% did not provide information on employment status.

Geographic diversity among all 34 studies included 112 locations; this researcher grouped similar locations into the following categories: hospitals (community, university, and VA), northeast Ohio retirement communities, clinics (primary care and specialty), cancer tumor registry, national surveys, community dwelling individuals, advertisements and referrals, and VA/Medicare claims (see Appendix B). The top three recruitment locations were 36 hospitals (32.1%), 29 northeast Ohio retirement communities (25.9%) and 28 clinics (25%). Twelve depression screening measures were used in these studies; some studies used more than one measure to assess depression. These measures include the BDI-II, CES-D, GDS, PHQ-9, SCID, SF-12/SF-36, DISH, 48-item symptom checklist (depression measured as a symptom), Hospital Anxiety and Depression Scale, MMPI-2, Cardiac

Depression Scale, and the MINI (Appendix C). The four most popular measures used to measure depression were the BDI-II (23.5% of studies), the CES-D (23.5% of studies), the GDS (11.8% of studies), and the PHQ-9 (11.8% of studies).

Seven (20.6%) of the 34 studies selected did not report the prevalence of depression among their collective 441,382 participants. In the remaining 27 studies, participants numbered 24,000. Of these, 73.7% (n=17,682) met criteria for either major or minor depression as measured by the utilized depression screening tools previously discussed. Of those individuals found to be depressed, 54.2% met eligibility for major depression and 45.8% showed symptoms of depression not severe enough to warrant a diagnosis of major depressive disorder. Depression alone did not entirely account for these 34 studies' findings; results were potentially influenced by several confounding factors (Appendix D). Few studies explored potential treatment methods; those that did evaluated psychotropic medication, cognitive behavioral therapy, COPD education, and dyspnea management.

Conclusions

Treatment cannot begin without recognition of the prevalence and severity of the problem. Depression and co-occurring chronic illness is a serious issue in our country today. Symptoms of depression are associated with disability and physical decline in older adults (Cho et al., 2010). Of the ten most common causes of death, 80% are due to chronic illness often accompanied with depression and/or anxiety (Livneh & Antonak, 2005). As mentioned above, this authors' study revealed that, in 27 studies with 24,000 participants diagnosed with at least one chronic illness, and 73.7% met criteria for either major or minor depression.

With numerous states around the country facing economic despair, individuals are at great risk for developing or deepening depression and, thus, speeding up the onset or worsening of chronic illness. Conversely, the number of individuals diagnosed with heart disease, lung disease, diabetes and cancer is on the rise as well, leading to the onset or worsening of depression. Either way, the utilization and cost of healthcare is directly affected by the decline of mental and physical health. The relationship between mental and physical health, the influence of psychological interventions on mental and physical health, and the potential of these interventions to reduce the cost of health care seem to be receiving very little attention in the country's current health care debates.

Effective coping skills need to be employed by individuals who struggle to manage their illness(es) due to symptoms of depression. Early screening and detection of depressive symptoms as well as recognizing potential risk factors (including a prior history of depression) play a key role in the development of psychological interventions that will empower individuals with effective coping skills (Livneh & Antonak, 2005; Cho et al., 2010). Medical and mental health professionals alike need to be aware of reliable and

171

valid measurement tools designed to screen for depression. Insurance companies need to understand the importance of covering ongoing mental health treatment in settings such as hospitals, skilled/long term care facilities, primary care clinics, specialty clinics and skilled home care especially when those insurance companies have increased their focus on outcomes in an effort to decrease costs.

The research discussed previously in Chapter Two demonstrates a positive relationship between depression and the management of chronic physical illness leading to additional struggles with poor social support, poor quality of life, anxiety, distress, poor coping skills, lack of control, poor self-efficacy and self-image, anger, stigma, self-blame and low self-esteem, suicidal ideation, increased utilization of healthcare services, and impending mortality. This researcher, through this study, investigated the relationship of depression with chronic physical illness, screening for depression, risk factors for developing depression, and potential psychological interventions. Answers to this study's research questions may potentially affect how and which services will be provided by medical and mental health professionals while supporting the fact that the utilization of effective psychological interventions would lower the cost of healthcare in the United States.

The following five research questions were explored for the purposes of this study. What relationship exists between chronic physical illness and symptoms of depression? What methods are used to screen for depressive symptoms and when is the best time to conduct screenings? What risk factors exist that predict the development of depression or depressive symptoms? And what psychological interventions affect symptoms of depression among individuals who have been diagnosed with or self-report at least one chronic illness? Is there a relationship between decreased symptoms of depression and decreased physical symptoms of chronic illness?

While all studies explored some aspect of the

173

relationship of depression to chronic illness, not all studies measured the prevalence of depression among their participants. Seven studies containing 441,382 participants did not report the prevalence of depression in their samples. Of those reporting depression, 54.2% of participants met eligibility for major depression and 45.8% reported symptoms of depression not severe enough for a diagnosis of major depressive disorder. To answer the first research question, there is a positive relationship between symptoms of depression and symptoms of chronic illness; as one increases or decreases, so does the other.

Fifteen studies investigating the reliability and validity of depressions screening tools revealed that, while diagnostic interviews are considered to be the gold standard for identifying depression, they are not well-suited to medical healthcare settings because interviews are time-consuming and clinicians need screenings to be brief (Merz et al., 2011). Self-report questionnaires have gained popularity as well because of how quickly they can be administered and scored. Some of the more popular self-report questionnaires for depression screening include the BDI-II, the CES-D, the GDS, and the PHQ-9 (all of which have been discussed in greater detail in Chapter Two and summarize previously in Chapter Three). Consistent with this report and answering the first half of the second research question, this study found that among the 12 measures used to screen for depression, the top four tools used in 34 studies were indeed the BDI-II (23.5% of studies), the CES-D (23.5% of studies), the GDS (11.8% of studies) and the PHQ-9 (11.8% of studies). In regards to second half of the second research question, the best time to screen for depression or depressive symptoms, most of the studies do not specifically measure a time frame, but most do express that it is best to screen patients for depression as early as possible.

Many patients, however, seem to be walking in and out of primary care settings and other healthcare settings with unnoticed and untreated depression. The third research question asks what risk factors exist that predict the development of depression. Only three studies included a focus on potential risk factors. These risk factors include functional impairment, poor health, perceived lack of social support, female, family history of mental illness, impoverishment, financial strain, significant life changes, pregnancy and post pregnancy, social isolation, somatic complaints, substance abuse, older age, loss of sex drive, chronic pain, diagnosis of two or more chronic illnesses, anxiety, anger, mental stress, and other psychosocial problems (Day et al., 2005; Maradiegue & Khan, 2013; Zauszniewski & Bekhet, 2009). As a result, this researcher recommends that if clinicians are aware of at least one risk factor, this is time to screen for depression.

Research questions four and five are related. What psychological interventions affect symptoms of depression among individuals who are diagnosed with or self-report at least one chronic illness and is there a relationship between decreased symptoms of depression and decreased physical symptoms of chronic illness? With the primary objective of this study being the investigation of the prevalence of depression in individuals with chronic illness, discovering potential psychological interventions would be evaluated if the selected studies addressed it as well as the prevalence of depression. Unfortunately, only two of the 34 studies examined potential interventions: cognitive behavioral therapy, COPD education and dyspnea management.

Kunik et al. (2008) found that participants showed significant improvement in BDI-II and BAI scores, improving walking distance, symptoms of anxiety and depression and quality of life significantly sustained over a period of 44 weeks. Likewise, Nguyen and Carrieri-Kohlman (2005) reported that dyspnea management accounted for significant improvement in CES-D scores from baseline to follow up two months later. To answer the research questions, these studies suggest that cognitive behavioral treatment, COPD education, and dyspnea management are potentially effective interventions for patients with chronic lung disease. Findings also show that, with these interventions, there is a positive relationship between both depressive symptoms and symptoms of chronic lung disease; as one decreases so does the other.

Based on the findings of this study, this researcher can conclude that there is a significant relationship between depression and chronic illness. The most popular measurement tools (BDI-II, CES-D, GDS, and PHQ-9) used by the majority of researchers to screen for depression have been proven to be reliable and valid measures. With a great number of potential risk factors for developing depression, patients should be screened for depression as early as possible; perhaps the best time is when clinicians recognize the presence of one to two risk factors. While there are a limited number of interventions utilized in these studies, chronic illness education, psychotropic medications, and cognitive behavioral therapies have the potential to decrease symptoms of depression; further investigation of effective interventions is critically needed.

Discussion

This study provides valuable insight not only into the importance of being aware of the prevalence of depression among adults with chronic illness but also of the need for effective treatments that provide relief from distressful depressive symptoms and lower utilization as well as costs of health care services. Though the above conclusions could easily be inferred from the findings of this study, results are not definitive. Many of the studies that reported the prevalence of depression only recruited participants already depressed, and nearly all participants had at least one chronic illness. Had these studies also had a control group of healthy (both physically and mentally) participants, the percentage of depressed individuals may have more closely matched the National Institute of Mental Health's (2011) statistics which state that one in four adults experience a mental health disorder. The researchers who administered treatments (cognitive behavioral therapy,

179

COPD, or dyspnea management) to small sample sizes cannot generalize results to any population except for individuals with depression and COPD in the geographic location in which they conducted their studies. Drawing definitive conclusions about the effect of these treatments on depressive symptoms is not possible for this reason and there are other potentially confounding factors that may have influenced study results.

Direction for Future Research

Researchers have two options for future investigations; either replicate previous studies and control for confounding factors, or pull out those confounding factors and create new research studies. However, before diving into either of these approaches, it is imperative to understand a more accurately assessed prevalence of co-morbid depression and chronic illness within the general population of the United States. To accomplish this, studies should focus on recruiting individuals to large random samples and dividing them into two groups:

individuals without a chronic illness and individuals with a chronic illness. Researchers need to utilize one or more of the top four screening tools (BDI-II, CES-D, GDS, PHQ-9) to measure depression and/or depressive symptoms in both groups. The questions to be asked must include the following: does the prevalence of depression or depressive symptoms in the non-chronically ill group agree or disagree with the findings of previous studies of the general population, and how does the prevalence of depression or depressive symptoms in the chronically ill group compare to the prevalence of depression or depressive symptoms in the non-chronically ill group?

The findings of this study suggest that the prevalence of depression or depressive symptoms should be higher in the chronically ill group than the non-chronically ill group, which, in turns, implies a significant impact on chronic illness and the utilization/cost of healthcare. This author also recommends that future research consider not only differences of depression or depressive symptoms based on gender, race/ethnicity, age, marital status, educational level and income status but also the utilization of healthcare services (hospitalization, doctor office visits, and reasons for seeking treatment). The literature reviewed for this study demonstrated that individuals who possess the following characteristics are at risk for developing depression or depressive symptoms: female, impoverished, financially strained, and older age. With these risk factors in mind, it will be helpful to the development of effective treatments of depression to understand the differences of depression or depressive symptoms among specific demographic groups.

After proving the relationship between depression and chronic illness and showing the differences of depression among demographic groups, future research must evaluate the impact of confounding factors. Studies that evaluate the influence of these confounds will make important contributions not only to effective treatment but also to the field of psychology. Physical symptoms like sleep quantity and quality, anxiety, and pain create a chain reaction effect potentially worsening depressive and chronic illness symptoms. The perception of control (i.e. an individual either believes or disbelieves he or she has the power to evoke change in their depressive or chronic illness symptoms) may also account for differences in depressive symptoms and warrants a closer look in future research.

Social isolation is noted as a risk factor for developing depression or depressive symptoms. However, the few studies that exist have conflicting findings supporting and rejecting the notion that social support affects severity of depression. Future research should evaluate all potential aspects of social support, including paid caregivers, friends and neighbors, and familial connections. Many people express that their faith, religion, or spirituality provides them with resources that help them cope with depression, chronic illness and other stressors. Exhaustive research is needed to show the relationship between faith/religion/spirituality and comorbid depression and chronic illness as the findings could have a significant impact on the approach to treatment. Self-image (how one views self), self-esteem (how well one likes self), and self-efficacy (how one views ability to effect change) may confound the results of studies seeking to understand the impact of depression on chronic illness as individuals with low self-image, low self-esteem, and/or low self-efficacy may not believe they can change how they feel both emotionally and physically.

Once research has provided an adequate understanding of the prevalence of depression or depressive symptoms among individuals with chronic illness, demonstrated the differences among demographic groups, and evaluated the impact of confounds and risk factors on comorbid depression and chronic illness, then additional future research should investigate numerous biopsychosocial treatment modalities. Education on disease management and progression as well as symptom recognition and control potentially influences not only chronic illness but also symptoms of depression. Exercise is known to release endorphins into the bloodstream that provide a calming effect on individuals experiencing significant stressors. Research that reviews the relationship between exercise, depression, and chronic illness could make significant strides in lowering the utilization of healthcare services.

Previous research suggested that effective treatment of depression and chronic illness should include the education of coping skills. Therefore, further research is needed that focuses solely on evaluating the effect of positive and negative coping skills on the alleviation or exacerbation of depressive symptoms. The most popular forms of treatment for depression are antidepressant medication and psychotherapy. If an individual's depression is truly caused by a chemical imbalance, then future research should be concerned with the effectiveness of psychotropic medication. Conversely, if an individual's depression is reactionary to the stress of life whether it is related to physical illness, family/marital discord, or other circumstances, then research that focuses on such therapies as cognitive behavior therapy, rational-emotive therapy, psychoanalysis, and behavioral therapy needs to investigate the success or failure of these models to treat depression and chronic illness.

When studies prove the connection between particular treatments and the successful management of depression and chronic illness, they, in essence, show the need for insurance companies to cover the provision of ongoing psychosocial therapy for their members. With the rise in the prevalence of depression, it is critical for clinicians to help individuals control their depression, which provides them with the ability (self-efficacy) to control their physical illness. As a result, appropriate psychological interventions have the potential to reduce the number of visits to the doctor's office, emergency room, and of hospital admissions while increasing an individual's ability to provide self-care (self-image and self-esteem). Research that provides health professionals with the tools for early detection and effective intervention of depression is important so that individuals with co-occurring depression and chronic physical illness will have greater quality of life.

References

American Cancer Society. (2010). Cancer facts and

figures. Retrieved from

http://www.cancer.org/acs/groups/content/@nho/doc

uments/document/acspc-024113.pdf

American Diabetes Association (ADA). (2011). Diabetes

basics: symptoms. Retrieved from

http://www.diabetes.org/diabetes-basics/symptoms/.

American Lung Association. (2011). Warning signs of lung

disease. Retrieved from

http://www.lungusa.org/your-lungs/signs-of-lung-

disease/.

American Psychiatric Association (APA). (2000). *Desk*

reference to the diagnostic criteria from DSM-IV-TR.

Washington D.C.: American Psychiatric Association.

Antai-Otong, D. (2007). The art of prescribing. *Perspectives*

in Psychiatric Care, 43(2), 93-96. Retrieved from

http://web.ebscohost.com.proxy1.calsouthern.edu/e

host/

pdfviewer/pdfviewer?vid=3&hid=7&sid=31300f19-
d557-481e-b33f-5f30dfe31ed2 %40sessionmgr15

Brown, L. M. & Schinka, J. A. (2005). Development and
initial validation of a 15-item informant version of the
geriatric depression scale. *International Journal of
Geriatric Psychiatry*, 20, 911-918.
doi:10.1002/gps.1375

Buck, C. J. (Ed.). (2009). *ICD-9-CM*. Canada: Saunders, an
imprint of Elsevier Inc.

Cannon, D. S., Tiffany, S. T., Coon, H., Scholand, M. B.,
McMahon, W. M., & Leppert, M. F. (2007). The
PHQ-9 as a brief assessment of lifetime major
depression. *Psychological Assessment,* 19(2), 247-
151. doi:10.1037/1040-3590.19.2.247

Carlson, M., Wilcox, R., Chou, C., Chang, M., Yang, F.,
Blanchard, J., Clark, F. (2011). Psychometric
properties of reverse-scored items on the CES-D in
a sample of ethnically diverse older adults.
Psychological Assessment, 23(2), 558-562.

doi:10.1037/a0022484

Centers for Disease Control. (2002). MMWR surveillance

summaries: Chronic obstructive pulmonary disease.

Retrieved from http://www.cdc.gov/media/

mmwrnews/n020802.htm.

Centers for Disease Control. (2009). Chronic disease . . .

the public health challenge of the 21st Century.

Retrieved from

http://www.cdc.gov/chronicdisease/pdf/2009-Power-

of-Prevention.pdf.

Centers for Disease Control. (2010). Cancer statistics by

cancer type. Retrieved from

http://www.cdc.gov/cancer/dcpc/data/types.htm.

Centers for Disease Control. (2010). Heart disease facts.

Retrieved from

http://www.cdc.gov/heartdisease/facts.htm.

Centers for Disease Control. (2010). High blood pressure

fact sheet. Retrieved from

http://www.cdc.gov/dhdsp/data_statistics/fact_sheet

s/fs_bloodpressure.htm

Centers for Disease Control. (2011). National chronic

kidney disease fact sheet. Retrieved from

http://www.cdc.gov/diabetes/pubs/pdf/kidney_Factsh

eet.pdf

Centers for Disease Control. (2011). National diabetes fact

sheet Retrieved from

http://www.cdc.gov/diabetes/pubs/pdf/ndfs_2011.pdf

Center for Managing Chronic Disease (CMCD). (2011).

What is chronic disease? Retrieved from

http://cmcd.sph.umich.edu/what-is-chronic-

disease.html

Chapman, D.P., Perry, G.S, & Strine, T.W. (2005). The vital

link between chronic disease and depressive

disorders. *Preventing Chronic Disease: Public*

Health Research, Practice, and Policy, 2(1), 1-10.

Retrieved from

http://www.cdc.gov/pcd/issues/2005/jan/04_0066.ht

m.

Chen, H., Baumgardner, D. J., & Rice, J. P. (2011). Health-related quality of life among adults with multiple chronic conditions in the United States, behavioral risk factors surveillance system, 2007. *Preventing Chronic Disease: Public Health Research, Practice, and Policy,* 8(1), 1-9. Retrieved from www.cdc.gov/pcd/issues/2011/jan/09_0234.htm

Chiu, C., Wray, L. A., Beverly, E. A., & Dominic, O. G. (2010). The role of health behaviors in mediating the relationship between depressive symptoms and glycemic control in type 2 diabetes: A structural equation modeling approach. *Social Psychiatry & Psychiatric Epidemiology,* 45, 67-76. doi:10.1007/s00127-009-0043-3

Cho, H. Y., Lavretsky, H., Olmstead, R., Levin, M., Oxman, M. N., & Irwin, M. R. (2010). Prior depression history and deterioration of physical health in community-dwelling older adults: A prospective cohort study. *The American Journal of Geriatric*

Psychiatry, 18(5), 442-251. Retrieved from

http://search.proquest.com/

docview/195990516?accountid=35183

Christensen, A. J. & Ehlers, S. L. (2002). Psychological

factors in end-stage renal disease: An emerging

context for behavioral medicine research. *Journal of*

Consulting and Clinical Psychology, 70(30, 712-724.

doi:10.1037//0022-006X.70.3.712

Cully, J. A., Graham, D. P., Stanley, M. A., Ferguson, C. J.,

Sharafkhaneh, A., Souchek, J., & Kunik, M. E.

(2006). Quality of life in patients with chronic

obstructive pulmonary disease and comorbid anxiety

or depression. *Psychosomatics,* 47(4), 312-319.

Retrieved from

http://web.ebscohost.com.proxy1.calsouthern.

edu/ehost/pdfviewer/pdfviewer?vid=3&hid=7&sid=fb

027c09-7c35-4ad7-a64d-

d068db8f63f1%40sessionmgr14

Cully, J. A., Phillips, L. L., Kunik, M. E., Stanley, M. A., &

Deswal, A. (2010). Predicting quality of life in

veterans with heart failure: The role of disease

severity, depression, and comorbid anxiety.

Behavioral Medicine, 36, 70-76.

doi:10.1080/08964280903521297

Daly, E. J., Trivedi, M. H., Raskin, P., & Grannemann, B. D.

(2007). Screening for depression in a diabetic

outpatient population. *International Journal of*

Psychiatry in Clinical Practice, 11(4), 268-272.

doi:10.1080/13651500701245981

Daniel, J., Honey, W., Landen, M., & Marshall-Williams, S.

(2003). Health risk behaviors and conditions among

persons with depression – New Mexico. *Morbidity*

and Mortality Weekly Report, 54(39), 989-991.

Retrieved from

http://search.proquest.com.proxy1.calsouthern.edu/p

qcentral/docview/203716310/fulltextPDF/1332EC35

915F1CF85B/2?accountid=35183

Day, R. C., Freedland, K. E., & Carney, R. M. (2005).

Effects of anxiety and depression on heart disease

attributions. *International Journal of Behavioral*

Medicine, 12(1), 24-29. Retrieved from

http://web.ebscohost.com.proxy1.

calsouthern.edu/ehost/pdfviewer/pdfviewer?vid=3&hi

d=7&sid=182bbbbb-a94d-4ee4-b943-

17ae18d807f3%40sessionmgr4

De Cock, E., Emons, W., Nefs, G., Pop, V., & Pouwer, F.

(2011). Dimensionality and scale properties of the

Edinburgh Depression Scale (EDS) in patients with

type 2 diabetes mellitus: the DiaDDzoB study. *BMC*

Psychiatry 2011, 11(141), 1-19. doi:10.1186/1471-

244X-11-141

DeCoster, V. A. & Cummings, S. M. (2005). Helping adults

with diabetes: A review of evidence-based

interventions. *Health & Social Work,* 30(3), 259-264.

Retrieved from

http://web.ebscohost.com.proxy1.calsouthern.edu/e

host/pdfviewer/

pdfviewer?vid=4&hid=7&sid=182bbbbb-a94d-4ee4-

b943-17ae18d807f3%40 sessionmgr4

Edwards, M. C., Cheavens, J. S., Heiy, J. E., & Cukrowicz,

K. C. (2010). A reexamination of the factor structure

of the Center for Epidemiologic Studies depression

scale: Is a one-factor model plausible?

Psychological Assessment, 22(3), 711-715.

doi:10.1037/a0019917

Else-Quest, N. M., LoConte, N. K., Shiller, J. H., & Hyde, J.

S. (2009). Perceived stigma, self-blame, and

adjustment among lung, breast, and prostate cancer

patients. *Psychology and Health,* 24(8), 949-964.

doi:10.1080/08870440802074664

Franks, H. M. & Roesch, S. C. (2006). Appraisals and

coping in people living with cancer: A meta-

analysis. *Psycho-Oncology,* 15, 1027-1037.

doi:10.1002/pon. 1043

Friedman, B., Heisel, M. J., & Delavan, R. L. (2005).

Psychometric properties of the 15-item geriatric

depression scale in functionally impaired, cognitively

intact, community-dwelling elderly primary care

patients. *Journal of the American Geriatrics Society,*

53, 1570-1576. doi:10.1111/j.1532-

5415.2005.53461.x

Grothe, K.B., Dutton, G.R., Jones, G.N., Bodenbos, J.,

Ancona, M., & Brantley, P.J. (2005). Validation of

the Beck Depression Inventory-II in a low-income

African American sample of medical outpatients.

Psychological Assessment, 17(1), 110-114.

doi:10.1037/1040-3590.17.1.110

Gruenberg, A. M., Goldstein, R. D. and Pincus, H. A.

(2008). *Classification of Depression: Research and*

Diagnostic Criteria: DSM-IV and ICD-10, in Biology

of Depression: From Novel Insights to Therapeutic

Strategies. Weinheim, Germany: Wiley-VCH Verlag

GmbH.

Hirsch, J. K., Duberstein, P. R., & Unützerm, J. (2009).

Chronic medical problems and distressful thoughts

of suicide in primary care patients: Mitigating role of happiness. *International Journal of Geriatric Psychiatry,* 24, 671-679. doi:10.1002/gps.2174

Hoth, K. F., Christensen, A. J., Ehlers, S. L., Raichle, K. A., & Lawton, W. J. (2007). A longitudinal examination of social support, agreeableness, and depressive symptoms in chronic kidney disease. *Journal of Behavioral Medicine,* 30(1), 69-76. doi:10.1007/s10865-006-9083-2

Hoyt, M. A., Thomas, K. S., Epstein, D. R., & Dirksen, S. R. (2009). Coping style and sleep quality in men with cancer. *Annals of Behavioral Medicine,* 37, 88-93. doi:10.1007/s12160-009-9079-6

Hu, J. & Gruber, K. J. (2008). Positive and negative affect and health functioning indicators among older adults with chronic illnesses. *Issues in Mental Health Nursing,* 29, 895-911. doi:10.1080/01612840802182938

Huffman, J. C., Smith, F. A., Quinn, D. K., & Fricchione, G.

L. (2006). Post-MI psychiatric syndromes: Six

unanswered questions. *Harvard Review of*

Psychiatry, 14(6), 305-318.

doi:10.1080/10673220601070013

Jerant, A., Chapman, B., Duberstein, P. & Franks, P.

(2010). Effects of personality on self-rated health in

a 1-year randomized controlled trial of chronic illness

self-management. *British Journal of Health*

Psychology, 15, 321-335.

doi:10.1348/135910709X464353

Kaholokula, J. K., Haynes, S. N., Grandinetti, A., & Chang,

H. K. (2006). Ethnic differences in the relationship

between depressive symptoms and health-related

quality of life in people with type 2 diabetes. *Ethnicity*

and Health, 11(1), 59-80.

doi:10.1080/13557850500391287

Karakus, M.C., & patton, L.C. (2011). Depression and the

onset of chronic illness in older adults: A 12-year

prospective study. *Journal of Behavioral Health*

Services, 38(3), 373-382.

Kellerman, Q. D., Christensen, A. J., Baldwin, A. S., & Lawton, W. J. (2010). Association between depressive symptoms and mortality risk in chronic kidney disease. *Health Psychology,* 29(6), 594-600. doi:10.1037/a0021235

Khalil, A. A., & Frazier, S. K. (2010). Depressive symptoms and dietary nonadherence in patients with end-stage renal disease receiving hemodialysis: A review of quantitative evidence. *Issues in Mental Health Nursing,* 31, 324-330. doi:10.3109/01612840903384008

Kirkova, J., Walsh, D., Rybicki, L., Davis, M. P., Aktas, A., Jin, T., & Homsi, J. (2010). Symptom severity and distress in advanced cancer. *Palliative Medicine,* 24(3), 330-339. doi:10.1177/0269216309356380

Kubzansky, L. D., Cole, S. R., Kawachi, I., Vokonas, P., & Sparrow, D. (2006). Shared and unique contributions of anger, anxiety, and depression to coronary heart disease: A prospective study in the

normative aging study. *Annals of Behavioral*

Medicine, 31(1), 21-29. Retrieved from

http://web.ebscohost.com.proxy1.

calsouthern.edu/ehost/pdfviewer/pdfviewer?vid=3&hi

d=21&sid=3a193e38-c738-402f-91dc-

6c8020cbb11d%40sessionmgr13

Kunik, M. E., Veazey, C., Cully, J. A., Souchek, J., Graham,

D. P., Hopko, D., Stanley, M. A. (2008). COPD

education and cognitive behavioral therapy group

treatment for clinically significant symptoms of

depression and anxiety in COPD patients: A

randomized controlled trial. *Psychological Medicine,*

38, 385-396. doi:10.1017/S0033291707001687

Lett, H. S., Blumenthal, J. A., Babyak, M. A., Catellier, D.

J., Carney, R. M., Berkman, L. S., Schneiderman, N.

(2009). Dimensions of social support and depression

in patients at increased psychosocial risk recovering

from myocardial infarction. *International Journal of*

Behavioral Medicine, 16, 248-258.

doi:10/1007/s12529-009-9040-x

Lichtenthal, W. G., Nilsson, M., Zhang, B., Trice, E. D.,

Kissane, D. W., Breitbart, W., & Prigerson, H. G.

(2009). Do rates of mental disorders and existential

distress among advanced-stage cancer patients

increase as death approaches? Psycho-Oncology,

18, 50-61. doi:10.1002/pon.1371

Livneh, H. & Antonak, R. F. (2005). Psychosocial

adaptation to chronic illness and disability: A primer

for counselors. Journal of Counseling &

Development, 83, 12-20. Retrieved from

http://web.ebscohost.com.proxy1.calsouthern.edu/e

host/

pdfviewer/pdfviewer?vid=3&hid=12&sid=9d12ec19-

da6f-40a4-8216d680cbfdd77 f%40sessionmgr4.

Lopez, M. N., Quan, N. M., & Carvajal, P. M. (2010). A

psychometric study of the geriatric depression scale.

European Journal of Psychological Assessment,

26(1), 55-60. doi:10/1027/1015-5759/a000008

Maradiegue, A.H., & Khan, F. (2013). Missed opportunities

in primary care: The importance of identifying

depression through screening, family history, &

chronic disease management. *Journal of*

Psychosocial Nursing, 51(2), 27-36.

doi:10.3928/02793695-20130109-04

Martens, M. P., Parker, J. C., Smarr, K. L., Hewett, J. E.,

Ge, B., Slaughter, J. R., & Walker, S. E. (2006).

Development of a shortened center for

epidemiological studies depression scale for

assessment of depression in rheumatoid arthritis.

Rehabilitation Psychology, 51(2), 135-139.

doi:10.1037/0090-5550.51.2.135

Merz, E. L., Malcarne, V. L., Roesch, S. C., Riley, N., &

Sadler, G. R. (2011). A multigroup confirmatory

factor analysis of the patient health questionnaire-9

among English- and Spanish-speaking Latinas.

Cultural Diversity and Ethnic Minority Psychology,

17(3), 309-316. doi:10.1037/a0023883

Morris, A., Yelin, E. H., Wong, B., & Katz, P. P. (2008).

Patterns of psychosocial risk and long-term

outcomes in rheumatoid arthritis. *Psychology,*

Health & Medicine, 13(5), 529-544.

doi:10.1080/13548500801927113

National Alliance on Mental Illness. (n.d.). What is mental

illness: Mental illness facts. Retrieved from

http://www.nami.org/template.cfm?section=About_M

ental_Illness.

National Alliance on Mental Illness. (2013). Mental illness

facts and numbers. Retrieved from

http://www.nami.org/factsheets/mentalillness_factsh

eet.pdf.

National Kidney Foundation. (2011). Chronic kidney

disease (CKD). Retrieved from

http://www.kidney.org/kidneydisease/ckd/index.cfm.

Nguyen, H. Q. & Carrieri-Kohlman, V. (2005). Dyspnea

self-management in patients with chronic obstructive

pulmonary disease: Moderating effects of

depressed mood. *Psychosomatics,* 46(5), 402-410.

Retrieved from http://psy.

psychiatryonline.org/cgi/reprint/46/5/402.

Paukert, A. L., LeMaire, A., & Cully, J. A. (2009). Predictors

of depressive symptoms in older veterans with heart

failure. *Aging & Mental Health,* 13(4), 601-610.

doi:10/1080/13607860802459823

Pudrovska, T. (2010). Why is cancer more depressing for

men than women among older white adults? *Social*

Forces, 89(2), 535-558. Retrieved from

http://content.ebscohost.com.proxy1.calsouthern.ed

u/pdf25_26/pdf/2010/SFR/01Dec10/57405559.pdf?T

=P&P=AN&K=57405559&S=R&D=pbh&EbscoConte

nt=dGJyMNHX8kSeprE4wtvhOLCmr0mep7FSr664T

LCWxWXS&ContentCustomer=dGJyMPGnrlG0p7JL

uePfgeyx44Dt6flA.

Quilty, L. C., Zhang, K. A., & Bagby, R. M. (2010). The

latent symptom structure of the Beck Depression

Inventory-II in outpatients with major depression.

Psychological Assessment, 22(3), 603-608.

doi:10.1037/a0019698

Rabkin, J. G., McElhiney, M., Moran, P., Acree, M., &

Folkman, S. (2009). Depression, distress and

positive mood in late-stage cancer: A longitudinal

study. *Psycho-Oncology,* 18, 79-86.

doi:10.1002/pon.1386

Roberts, R. E., Kaplan, G. A., Shema, S. J., & Strawbridge,

W. J. (1997). Prevalence and correlates of

depression in an aging cohort: The Alameda county

study. *The Journals of Gerontology*, 52B(5), S252-

S258. Retrieved from http://

deepblue.lib.umich.edu/bitstream/2027.42/51564/1/

Roberts%20RE,%20Prevalence%20and%20Correla

tes%20of%20Depression%20in%20an%20Aging%2

0Cohort,%201997.pdf.

Roesch, S. C., Adams, L., Hines, A., Palmores, A., Vyas,

P., Tran, C., Vaughn, A. A. (2005). Coping with

prostate cancer: A meta-analytic review. *Journal of Behavioral Medicine, 28*(3), 281-293. doi:10.1007/s10865-005-4664

Rybarczyk, B., Grady, K. L., Naftel, D. C., Kirklin, J. K., White-Williams, C., Kobashigawa, J., Higgins, R. (2007). Emotional adjustment 5 years after heart transplant: A multisite study. *Rehabilitation Psychology, 52*(2), 206-214. doi:10.1037//0090-5550.52.2.206

Sacco, W. P. & Yanover, T. (2006). Diabetes and depression: The role of social support and medical symptoms. *Journal of Behavioral Medicine, 29*(6), 523-531. doi:10.1007/s10865-006-9072-5

Schlegel, R. J., Talley, A. E., Molix, L. A., & Bettencourt, B. A. (2009). Rural breast cancer patients, coping and depressive symptoms: A prospective comparison study. *Psychology and Health, 24*(8), 933-948. doi:10.1080/0887044080225 4613

Shen, C., Findley, P., Banerjea, R., & Sambamoorthi, U.

(2010). Depressive disorders among cohorts of women veterans with diabetes, heart disease, and hypertension. *Journal of Women's Health,* 19(8), 1475-1486. doi:10.1089/ jwh.2009.1551

Scogin, F. & Shah, A. (2006). Screening older adults for depression in primary care settings. *Health Psychology,* 25(6), 675-677. doi:10.1037/0278-6133.25.6.675

Theis, K. A., Helmick, C. G., & Hootman, J. M. (2007). Arthritis burden and impact are greater among U.S. women than men: Intervention opportunities. *Journal of Women's Health,* 16(4), 441-453. doi:10.1089/jwh.2007.371

Thomas, J. L. & Brantley, P. J. (2004). Factor structure of the Center for Epidemiologic Studies Depression Scale in low-income women attending primary care clinics. *European Journal of Psychological Assessment,* 20(2), 106-115. doi:10.1027/1015-5759.20.2.106

Walker, M. S., Zona, D. M., & Fisher, E. B. (2006).

Depressive symptoms after lung cancer surgery:

Their relation to coping style and social support.

Psycho-Oncology, 15, 684-693.

doi:10.1002/pon.997

Wall, M. P. (2007). Predictors of functional performance in

community-dwelling people with COPD. *Journal of*

Nursing Scholarship, 29(3), 222-228.

doi:10.1111/j.1547-5069.2007.00172.x

Wancata, J., Alexandrowicz, R., Marquart, B., & Friedrich,

F. (2006). The criterion validity of the Geriatric

Depression Scale: A systematic review. *Acta*

Psychiatrica Scandinavica, 114, 398-410.

doi:10.1111/j.1600-0447.2006. 00888.x

Wiebe, J. S. & Penley, J. A. (2005). A psychometric

comparison of the Beck Depression Inventory-II in

English and Spanish. *Psychological Assessment,*

17(4), 481-485. doi:10.1037/1040-3590.17.4.481

Williams, R. T., Heinemann, A. W., Bode, R. K., Wilson, C.

S., Fann, J. R., & Tate, D. G. (2009). Improving

measurement properties of the Patient Health

Questionnaire-9 with rating scale analysis.

Rehabilitation Psychology, 54(2), 198-203.

doi:10.1037/a00155529

Zauszniewski, J. A. & Bekhet, A. K. (2009). Depressive

symptoms in elderly women with chronic conditions:

Measurement issues. *Aging & Mental Health,* 13(1),

64-72. doi:10.1080/13607860802154481

Zautra, A. J., Parrish, B. P., Van Puymbroeck, C. M.,

Tennen, H., Davis, M. C., Relch, J. W., Irwin, M.

(2007). Depression history, stress, and pain in

rheumatoid arthritis patients. *Journal of Behavioral*

Medicine, 30, 187-197. doi:10.1007/s10865-007-

9097-4

Appendix A: Summary of Demographics

Table 1

Summary of Demographics (N=465,382; 34 Studies)

Demographic		Number of Studies	Number of Participants	Percentage of studies (%)†	Percentage of Subjects (%)†
Race/Ethnicity					
	Total Reporting	28	453,881	82.4	97.5
	Not Available	6	11,501	17.6	2.5
	Caucasian/White	28	314,086	82.4	69.2
	Minorities	28	139,795	82.4	30.8
Gender					
	Total Reporting	32	465,143	94.1	99.9
	Not Available	2	199	5.9	0.1
	Female	32	242,805	94.1	52.2
	Male	32	222,338	94.1	47.8
Marital Status					
	Total Reporting	19	451,359	55.9	97
	Not Available	15	14,023	44.1	3
	Married/Partner	19	272,169	55.9	60.3
	Not Married	19	179,190	55.9	39.7
Education					
	Total Reporting	16	438,926	47.1	94.3
	Not Available	11	24,742	32.4	5.3
	Mean Ed.*	7	1,714	20.6	0.4
	High School and Greater than HS	16	388,738	47.1	88.6
	Less than HS	16	50,106	47.1	11.4
Income					
	Total Reporting	14	436,385	41.2	93.8
	Not Available	20	26,860	58.8	5.8
	Mean Income**	2	2,024	5.9	0.4
	Median Income***	2	113	5.9	0.1
	< $10,000	1	145	2.9	0.03
	> $10,000	1	8	2.9	0
	$10-20,000	1	40	2.9	0.01
	<$10,000 & > $20,000	1	56	2.9	0.01
	< $20,000	2	2020	5.9	0.5
	> $20,000	2	1724	5.9	0.4
	< $25,000	2	94,841	5.9	21.7
	> $25,000	2	336,209	5.9	77.0
	< $30,000	2	532	5.9	0.1
	> $30,000	2	345	5.9	0.07
	Employed	2	168	5.9	0.03
	Not Employed	2	276	5.9	0.06

*Range of Mean Education is 12.4-15.15 years.
** Mean Incomes are $37,171 & $35-35,000
***Median Incomes are $25,000 & $20-30,000
†Percentages may equal more than 100% due to rounding

Appendix B: Geographic Diversity

Table 2

Geographic Locations for Recruitment (N=112 in 8 groups; 34 Studies)

Location	Number of Locations	Percentage of Locations (%)
Hospitals (Community, VA, University)	36	32.1
Northeast Ohio Retirement Communities	29	25.9
Clinics (Primary Care & Specialty)	28	25.0
Cancer Tumor Registry	9	8.0
National Surveys	6	5.4
Community Dwelling Individuals	2	1.8
Ads & Referrals	1	0.9
VA & Medicare Claims	1	0.9

Appendix C: Depression Screening Tools

Table 3

Use of Depression Screening Tools (N=34 Studies)

Measure	Number of Studies Using Measure	Percentage of Studies Using Measure (%)†
BDI-II	8	23.5
CES-D	8	23.5
GDS	4	11.8
PHQ-9	4	11.8
SCID	3	8.8
SF-12 or SF-36	3	8.8
DISH	2	5.9
48 Symptom Checklist	1	2.9
Hospital Anxiety and Depression Scale	1	2.9
MMPI-2	1	2.9
Cardiac Depression Scale	1	2.9
MINI	1	2.9

†Percentages will be greater than 100% because some studies used more than one screening tool to measure depression.

Appendix D: Potential Confounding Factors

Depression and Chronic Illness Studies (8)
- Positive or Negative Affect
- Symptom Distress
- Healthcare Functioning
- Quality of Life
- Happiness
- Neuroticism
- Distress from Suicidal Ideation
- Personality
- Self-Rated Health
- General Health
- Mental Distress
- Physical Distress
- Activity Limitations

Depression and Cancer Studies (6)
- Approach of Death
- Complicated Grief
- Terminal Illness Acknowledgement
- Religiousness/Spirituality
- Suicidality
- Coping Skills
- Optimism
- Social Support
- Denial
- Functional Ability
- Sleep Quality
- Self-Efficacy
- Physical Impact of Cancer
- Functional Support
- Masculinity Beliefs
- Sexual Activity

Depression and Heart Disease Studies (6)
        Social Support
        Agreeableness
        Quality of Life
        Anxiety
        Health Interventions
        Physical Limitations
        Intrusiveness of Illness on Lifestyle
        Coping Skills
        Locus of Control
        Self-Efficacy
        Anger
        Emotional Adjustment
        Positive and Negative Affect
        Sickness Impact

Depression and Diabetes/Chronic Kidney Disease
Studies (6)
        Social Support
        Agreeableness
        Quality of Life
        Functional Ability
        Symptoms
        Subjective Health
        Mortality
        Health Behaviors
        Glycemic Control
        Ethnicity

Depression and Cancer Studies (8)
        Distress
        Positive Mood
        Stigma
        Self-Blame
        Self-Esteem
        Anxiety
        Anger
        Causal Attributes

Symptom Severity
Performance
Severity of Illness
Quality of Life

Depression and Arthritis Studies (3)
Pain
Perceived Stress
Positive Affect
Number of Doctor Visits
Perceived Ability to Cope
Perceived Impact of Illness
Social Support
Psychological Mastery
Satisfaction with Health & Functioning

Depression and Lung Disease Studies (4)
Cognitive Behavioral Therapy
COPD Education
Anxiety
Quality of Life
Physical Functioning
Physiologic Well-Being
Comorbidity & Severity of Disease
Coping Resources
Social Support & Mastery
Well-Being
Happiness
Life Satisfaction
Dyspnea Severity
Exercise
Social Functioning

About Valerie S. Brandal, Psy.D.

Dr. Brandal grew up in rural Northern Michigan the oldest of four children and graduated from Evart Public Schools. She moved to Grand Rapids where she lived for 15 years, graduating from Grand Rapids Baptist College in 1994 with a Bachelor of Arts degree (majors: music and psychology, minor: Christian Ministries) and from Western Michigan University in 2005 with a Master of Social Work degree.

Dr. Brandal has internship experiences in music therapy, youth residential treatment, gerontology, and youth counseling through the Franciscan Life Process Center in Lowell, Wedgwood Christian Services and Gerontology Network Services both in Grand Rapids. Her work experiences include direct care, program manager, and nursing home social work with Hope Network Behavioral Health Services, Arbor Circle's The Bridge, and Heartland Healthcare Center, all in Grand Rapids.

Dr. Brandal moved back to Northern Michigan in 2004 to be closer to family. She currently works as a medical social worker for Mercy Home Care Mercy Hospice (which will soon be Munson Home Health on February 1, 2015) in Cadillac, traveling across 12 counties to assess the psychosocial needs of home bound individuals and families. Dr. Brandal successfully defended her doctoral project on October 31, 2013 being bestowed immediately with the title of doctor and was awarded her Doctor of Psychology diploma on January 16, 2014.